MW01101104

FREEDOM FIGHTER

Freedom is the last, best hope of earth.
—Abraham Lincoln

FREEDOM FIGHTER

How God wins the universal war on terror

Ken Wilson
with Kelley Lorencin

Elathia Press, Michigan

ISBN: 978-0-578-02033-4

Published by Elathia Press, Michigan

Cover design by Chris Wilson
Cover picture © istockphoto.com/Zirafek
Cover prepared for printing by Sans Serif, Inc.

Printed in the United States of America by Malloy, Inc.

Additional copies of this book are available at www.freedomfighterbook.com

Scripture quotations marked *Message* are taken from The Message. Copyright © 1993, 1994, 1995, 1996, 2000, 2001, 2002. Used by permission of NavPress Publishing Group.

Scripture quotations marked NCV are taken from the New Century Version. Copyright © 2005 by Thomas Nelson, Inc. Used by permission. All rights reserved.

Scripture quotations marked NLT are taken from the Holy Bible, New Living Translation, copyright © 1996, 2004. Used by permission of Tyndale House Publishers, Inc., Wheaton, Illinois 60189. All rights reserved.

Scripture quotations marked NIV are taken from the HOLY BIBLE, NEW INTERNA-TIONAL VERSION®. Copyright © 1973, 1978, 1984 International Bible Society®. Used by permission of Zondervan. All rights reserved.

Scripture quotations marked TNIV are taken from the HOLY BIBLE, TODAY'S NEW INTERNATIONAL VERSION®. Copyright © 2001, 2005 by International Bible Society®. Used by permission of International Bible Society®. All rights reserved worldwide.

For my beautiful wife, Joyce,

who encouraged me daily in the writing of this book

and gave me our three incredible gifts from God:

Chris, Kelley, and Claire

Contents

Acknowledgements

A word of thanks

I believe you should study the Bible for yourself, but not *by yourself.*
I want to thank my Bible study group of twenty-four years and my
classes of students for their insights and questions. This book represents some emergent conclusions that have taken shape over a lifetime of experience and study with these groups.

Any farsighted ideas you may find here are the result of my
having stood on the shoulders of giants, as Newton once put it. I'm
happy to identify those who have been giants in my life: Dr. Graham Maxwell, Dr. Helmut Thielicke, C.S. Lewis, Dr. Jack Provon-
sha, Ellen G. White, Dr. Eugene Petersen, Dr. Alden Thompson,
and J.B. Phillips.

Most of all, I am indebted to my daughter Kelley, who took
the skeletal bones of my notes and put the flesh of clarity and interest on them. Without her, these bones would have remained dry and
disconnected.

Introduction

What this book is about

One day, an undergraduate student at Harvard burst into Chaplain Harry Emerson Fosdick's office and announced that he did not believe in God. Dr. Fosdick asked him to sit down and said, "Tell me about the God you say does not exist."

He listened attentively as the young man spoke about his atheism. When he was finished, Dr. Fosdick looked at him kindly and said, "If I thought that God was like that, I wouldn't believe he existed either."

That was a turning point for the young man. This book is that sort of statement. It is the confession of a lifelong Bible teacher and friend of the God revealed in that Bible. It is the reflection of the God that I have come to know, the God who really does exist.

The universal war on terror

Crisis in God's creation

Only when we are no longer afraid do we begin to live.
—*Dorothy Thompson*

You live in a war zone. No matter what continent you live on, no matter what country you're from, no matter your nationality, religion, language, or race, you live on a battlefield. But this is no ordinary war. There are no bombs, bullets, tanks, or planes. In the hustle and bustle of everyday life, this is an invisible war—a war being fought for the hearts and minds of God's intelligent beings. This is a war of propaganda and fear. For centuries, God has been fighting a war on terror.

Imagine that you live in a small, isolated town. There is one doctor in this town, and he has just told you that you have an aggressive form of deadly cancer. Without treatment, you'll be dead in a matter of weeks. Fortunately, he says he has a formula that will cure you and restore you to perfect health. In addition, he claims that if you take this treatment, you will live a long and prosperous life and never be sick again. There's just one catch: his treatment contains cyanide.

Cyanide? you think. *Isn't that a deadly poison?* Concerned, you question the doctor. You desperately want to be healthy, but it's hard to believe that cyanide will help. The doctor assures you that everything will be just fine if you follow his instructions.

Would you drink the cyanide?

Wouldn't your decision be based on whether you trusted the doctor or not? If you and the doctor were friends, you would trust him to help you. But what if you believed the doctor wanted to get rid of you? What if you'd heard a rumor that he was looking for a chance to kill you? Would you be willing to drink his cyanide treatment then?

I wouldn't, and I'm willing to bet that you wouldn't either. In fact, you might even question whether his diagnosis was true.

Trust. This is the issue at the center of the war that is raging in the universe. But this war is not about a doctor. It's about God.

Can we trust God? This is the question at the heart of the universal war on terror. It's a question God has been answering for many centuries. Maybe it seems like it should be an easy question to answer. But it has taken us a long time to reach a conclusion because we can't see or think clearly. On this planet, our minds are clouded with something called "sin."

Sin is a rebellious attitude that comes from distrusting God. It is like a disease. Just as cancer grows from a single cell into something that can destroy you, sin starts small and eventually gets big and ugly. If it isn't healed, it will break our connection to God, the source of life. Breaking that connection leads to death.

When a lamp is unplugged, the light goes out. This is what happens to a person who has severed his connection with God. His life "goes out." Sin is dangerous because it causes death.[1] That's why God warns us to stay away from it.

Our planet hasn't always been full of sin. In fact, God created Earth to be a paradise. During creation week, he planted a beautiful garden—the Garden of Eden. Then, he created the first humans—Adam and Eve—and put them in the garden. Everything he made was perfect. God intended it to be that way forever.

Unfortunately, things didn't stay perfect for very long. Sin entered our world through Adam and Eve. They "sinned" when they decided not to trust God.*

God had asked them not to eat the fruit of a certain tree in the garden where they lived. They were free to eat from any other

---

* You can read all about that in Genesis, chapter 3.

tree, but not the Tree of the Knowledge of Good and Evil.[2] God told them they would die if they ate the fruit of that tree.

One day, Eve met a serpent at that very tree who told her that she shouldn't trust God. The serpent said God was a liar. The serpent said the fruit wasn't deadly. In fact, the serpent told Eve that if she and Adam ate the fruit, they would be as powerful as God.

Eve believed the serpent. She believed God had been lying to her. She decided she wanted to be as powerful as God. So, she took matters into her own hands and ate the fruit.

When she took some of the fruit to her husband, Adam, he was shocked. He was sure Eve had done the wrong thing by eating the fruit. He believed she was going to die because she had eaten it, and he couldn't bear to live without her. So, Adam also decided not to trust God. He took matters into his own hands, and he ate the fruit.

Adam and Eve's choice to distrust God *immediately* led to fear. After they ate the fruit, they hid from God when he came walking through the garden looking for them. After God found them and asked Adam why he was hiding, Adam admitted that he was afraid.[3]

Like a genetic disease, Adam and Eve passed on this distrust and fear of God to their children. And their children passed it on to their children. And so it has continued down through the ages. This fear of God has infected the gene pool of the human race. It affects every person who has ever been born.

God wants to restore our trust in him so we won't be afraid of him anymore. That's why he's fighting this war on terror. The "terror" God is fighting against is our fear of him! For centuries, he has been laying out all the evidence for us. He wants us to make an informed decision about whether or not we can trust him.

The enemy in this war claims that God is someone to be afraid of. Adam and Eve believed the enemy and went on the run. We've been on the run from God ever since.

At some point, Lucifer decided he wanted to be "number one." He set out to take control of the universe. Of course, he knew he couldn't accomplish this by force. He knew he wasn't as powerful as God. He must have figured that God would quickly squash any open rebellion. So he decided to overthrow God's government with a revolution instead.

He began to tell lies about God to the other angels. Instead of openly opposing God, he planted seeds of doubt and distrust. He told them what he later told Adam and Eve: "You can't really trust God." He said God was arbitrary, unjust, and unfair. These ideas had never before entered the minds of God's angels. They must have wondered: *Could Lucifer be telling the truth? He is God's trusted messenger. He knows God better than any of us! Is God really like this?*

That's how the war began. When Revelation says there was war in heaven, it doesn't mean a bloody war with bombs and bullets. Instead, it was (and still is) a war of ideas about the kind of person God really is.

After the war began in heaven, Lucifer became known as Satan,* which means *enemy*. He is God's primary opponent in this universal war on terror. He wants us all to be afraid of God. Revelation mentions him as the tormentor of this earth: "He is that old

---

* Derived from the Hebrew word for "accuser." For the sake of clarity, from this point on, we will refer to him as "Satan" instead of "Lucifer."

snake called the devil, or Satan, who tricks the whole world. It will be terrible for the earth and the sea, because the devil has come down to you! He is filled with anger, because he knows he does not have much time."[2]

This is something that many people don't realize: God created our planet *after* the war began. In a universe where a war was raging, Earth was a paradise, a peaceful oasis. But it wasn't long before Satan came to our planet, hoping to corrupt us. He wanted to hurt God by spoiling our happiness. He wanted to destroy our trust in God and ruin our paradise.

It worked. Adam and Eve's decision to distrust God plunged the human race into spiritual misery. What began as joy and happiness quickly turned to guilt and fear. Instead of finding freedom, power, and joy in eating the fruit, Adam and Eve found slavery, weakness, and pain. Because of their decision, we're stuck right in the middle of the war.

Battlefield Earth

The war continues

The ordinary man is an anarchist. He wants to do as he likes. He may want his neighbor to be governed, but he himself doesn't want to be governed.
——*George Bernard Shaw*

Centuries after Adam and Eve's decision to believe Satan instead of God, the prophet Isaiah* wrote that the inhabitants of this planet were "people walking in darkness."[1]

Isaiah didn't mean that the sun had stopped shining. He was talking about spiritual darkness. That kind of darkness comes from not knowing if we can trust God.

---

* The prophet Isaiah was born in the eighth century BC, seven hundred years before the birth of Jesus. He prophesied during the reigns of Uzziah, Jotham, Ahaz, and Hezekiah. Scholars believe he died as a martyr at the hands of King Manasseh, who sawed him in half with a wooden saw. He authored Isaiah, one of the Old Testament books of the Bible.

We may not know it, but deep down inside, we're afraid of God. We're not really sure what he's like. We lurch and stumble around in the darkness, wondering if God is a monster or a tyrant.

Even when we say "God is love," our hidden beliefs about him don't always line up with our words. For instance, many Christians believe that God sent his Son, Jesus Christ, to "die in our place." What does that mean? With flowery language, many explain that God the Father was going to kill us because of our sin. However, he made a plan to kill his Son instead so he could save us. Many Christians also believe that if anyone rejects this gift of salvation, God will kill them anyway or burn them in hell forever.

What do such beliefs say about God? Wouldn't you be afraid of someone who was out to kill you? Would you try to be friends with someone who wanted you dead? These hidden beliefs expose our fear of God.

We may have constructed intricate "theologies" to deal with this fear, but it's still there. In our hearts, we're still afraid. We still believe God is out to get us. Consequently, we are *so grateful* for Jesus and his sacrifice. But, without Jesus in the way, we wouldn't even think of approaching God!

Six thousand years after Adam and Eve hid from God in the Garden of Eden, we're still hiding from him. But even if our fear is irrational, it's still a reality. So how can God overcome it? If we *shouldn't* be afraid of God, how can he convince us of that while we're running away from him? How can he change our minds? How can he coax us out of hiding?

Thank goodness Isaiah went on to say that the people walking in darkness "have seen a great light. On those living in the land of the shadow of death, a light has dawned."² This light was Jesus.

God himself came to our little, messed-up paradise to show us the truth about what he's like. He became a human being—one of us! He moved right into the neighborhood and lived with us. That way, we could get to know what he is really like without being afraid of him.

Satan said God was unkind, but Jesus showed us that God is actually compassionate. Satan said God was a liar, but Jesus showed us that God actually speaks the truth. Satan said God was a tyrant, but Jesus showed us that God is actually patient. Satan said God was selfish, but Jesus showed us that God actually cares more about the needs of others.

Satan lied to us about God's character. In Jesus, however, we see what God is really like. And the truth about him is a great, shining light that "the darkness can never extinguish."³ God wants this light to coax us out of hiding and bring us home to him.

Jesus once told a story about a father who had two sons. One of those sons decided to leave his family forever. He demanded his share of the family fortune and ran away with it. He quickly squandered everything he had. He ended up as a poor, dirty slave. His job was to feed his master's pigs, and he lived with the pigs in the pigpen. He was so hungry, he thought about eating the pig slop.

Then, something happened: "When he finally came to his senses, he said to himself, 'At home even the hired servants have food enough to spare, and here I am dying of hunger!'"[4]

Do you see what happened? The boy had a revelation about the character of his father. He was a dirty, starving slave, and suddenly he realizes: *My father doesn't treat his servants like this! My father is a good man with a kind and generous heart. My father's servants never go hungry.* This revelation about his father caused the boy to get up and go home.[†]

This is our story too. By eating the fruit, Adam and Eve plunged us all into the pigpen. They made us slaves to sin, and Satan has seen to it that we are dirty and starving. He is a harsh and cruel master. He wants us to believe we're stuck. He wants us to be too ashamed and afraid to go home.

But God has a different plan. Instead of punishing us for our rebellion, he has given us a revelation about his character. He

[†] Jesus must have loved good stories with shocking twists at the end. Read Luke 15:18-31 to discover what happened when the boy went home.

has shown us that he is a good God with a kind, generous heart and a forgiving spirit. He doesn't want us to be afraid. He wants us to come home.

This is the war. Can we trust God or not? You decide. The answer is in his character.

Inner Beauty

God's internal characteristics

God's character begins with his internal qualities.

These personal traits define his nature, essence, and being.

God didn't "decide" to be this way.

These traits are inherent in his very nature.

Thus, these qualities are eternal and unchanging.

If you've seen one, you've seen 'em all

God's oneness

Let there be such oneness between us that when one cries, the other tastes salt.
—*Unknown*

Unity. Belonging. Identity. These concepts resonate with us on some level. In some way, each of us seeks to be "at one" with something else. We might seek this through marriage, meditation, friendship, a local book club, gang initiation, church fellowship, sex, academic pursuit, or any number of things. Somewhere inside all of us is the need to align ourselves with someone or something else. This need is a reflection of God's image in us.

The God who created this world exists in an eternal unity of three persons.* Trying to explain this is like trying to describe the way a baby develops in the womb. We can observe and describe

---

* This unit is often called "the Trinity."

each step in the process, but we can't *really explain* how it works or why it happens in the first place.

God is three, and God is one. This idea has stumped philosophers and theologians for centuries. Nevertheless, it is crucial to understanding the beauty of God's character—just as it is crucial to understand that children come from their mothers' wombs and are not flown in by the stork.

God Is Three

Saying that "God is three" means that in the person of God, there are three beings: a Father, a Son, and a Spirit. These three beings assume different roles in God's relationship to all created things:

The Father is the creator and sustainer of all life. The sovereign of the universe, he reigns supreme in power and majesty over every living creature. We might think of him as "The Big Guy Upstairs."

The Son is better known to us as Jesus Christ. Fully God and fully man, he lived on this planet two thousand years ago. In fact, his existence with us divided history. (Before his birth, time was measured in years BC. After his birth, time is measured in years AD.) He is the divine "media department." He communicates to created beings about God.

The Spirit interacts in a very intimate way with us. The Bible calls the human body the "temple of the Holy Spirit."[1] The Spirit literally lives inside of us. He inspires, encourages, corrects, renews, and transforms us from within.

God Is One

Saying that "God is one" means that these three beings are *identical* in character, purpose, motivation, and essential nature. Though the Father, Son, and Spirit serve different roles, each one perfectly mirrors and represents the others. Each is eternal, all-powerful, all-knowing, and ever-present. All three exist in a state of perfect harmony, agreement, and love.

Jesus tried to explain this oneness to his disciples.† They had asked Jesus to tell them about "The Big Guy Upstairs." Even though the disciples had lived with Jesus for three years, they wanted to know what the Father was like. And Jesus said, "If you really knew me, you would know my Father as well. From now on, you *do know him*. You've even *seen him! To see me is to see the Father.*"[2]

According to Jesus, we don't have to wonder what the Father and Spirit are like. We've *seen* the Father because we've seen the Son. We *know* the Spirit because we know the Son.

---

† The disciples were a group of twelve men who were taught in a special way by Jesus when he lived on Earth. Jesus had chosen them to become his core group. He discussed ideas with them and spent time with them. They called him *rabbi*, or teacher.

This is one of the earliest and clearest statements about God made in the Bible: "Hear, O Israel: The Lord our God, the Lord is one."[3] The Father, Son, and Spirit are *one*. They do not contradict one another. They do not manipulate or pacify one another. They do not plead with one another. This means that if either the Father or the Spirit had come in person to this earth instead of Jesus, history would be no different. We would have witnessed the same love, compassion, and sympathy we saw in Jesus.

Isaiah got a glimpse of this when he wrote about the time when Jesus would come to Earth. Here is his marvelous description of that event: "For to us a child is born, to us a son is given, and the government will be on his shoulders. And he shall be called Wonderful Counselor, Mighty God, Everlasting Father, Prince of Peace."[4]

Do you see how Isaiah lays out the three-in-one essence of God in this passage? Our *Mighty God* includes an *Everlasting Father*, a *Prince of Peace*, and a *Wonderful Counselor*. And Isaiah said that Jesus would be called *all of them*. He prophesied that God in all three persons would be present in the life of Jesus. The only way that can be true is if God is one.

This is great news for those of us who like Jesus, but tend to be afraid of "The Big Guy Upstairs." Imagine this: the Father is just as loving and forgiving as the Son. The Father is just as compassionate and encouraging as the Spirit. We may come to the Father freely and without fear. We may come to the Father as easily as we come to Jesus.

Jesus doesn't have to stand between the Father and us. He doesn't have to "plead our case" to the Father. In fact, Jesus plainly said that he *wouldn't* plead with the Father for us.[5] The Father and Spirit love us just as much as Jesus does. All three share the same compassionate heart and creative spirit.

Jesus, the divine "media department," said that if we had seen one, we had seen 'em all. He wants us to know that *every* character trait we admire in him applies *equally* and *without exception* to the Father and the Spirit!

Life preserver

God's immortality

*Work hard for sin your whole life and your pension is death. But God's gift is
real life, eternal life, delivered by Jesus, our Master.*
—*Paul, the apostle* [1]

Have you ever noticed that we live in a society obsessed with staying
alive? We funnel money into medical research, trying to find cures
for diseases. We continually develop technology to improve health-
care. We strive for more effective disease prevention and treatment.

We try to keep our children safe from everything. We practi-
cally outfit them in body armor before they ride their bikes around
the block. We teach them to be skeptical of everything and warn
them to stay away from strangers. We give them all the right vacci-
nations and continually disinfect their little environments. We take
all the proper safety precautions.

Every time we hear of a new threat to our wellness, we attempt to squash it. We stop eating dairy products because of the hormones. We stop buying regular produce because of the pesticides. We stop drinking tap water. We buy the safest cars, and we outfit our homes with state-of-the-art security systems.

We're obsessed.

Have you also noticed, however, that—in this society obsessed with staying alive—people die every day? There's no escaping it. No matter what strategies we adopt in our quest for a longer life, we frequently discover that we don't have all the control. The person who eats a strict vegan diet is killed by a drunk driver. The person who refuses to fly is killed by a silent brain aneurism. The child who always wears a bicycle helmet is killed by a crazy gunman at his school.

We can't outrun death on this planet. No matter how badly we want to stay alive, we are all going to die. No matter how carefully we try to avoid tragedy, we will all stop breathing someday. This isn't a threat. It's just a fact. We can't create or sustain life. At some point, we must realize that we are ultimately dependent on something outside ourselves for existence.

Instead of feeling worried or depressed about this, we should rejoice, because the Bible tells us where life comes from. God has it. In fact, life is found *only* in God. Jesus said, "I came to give life—life in all its fullness."[2] Elsewhere, he said, "I am the way, the truth, and the life."[3]

The apostle John,* one of Jesus's disciples, picked up on this concept. In the opening passage of the Gospel of John, he describes God as the source of life: "In the beginning, the Word *already existed.* The Word was with God, and the Word was God. He existed in the beginning with God. God created everything through him, and nothing was created except through him. The Word *gave life to every-thing* that was created, and his life brought light to everyone."[4]

What an incredible thought! John says that in the beginning—before there was a single planet, star, plant, galaxy, animal, or person—God existed. In the beginning, he was already there. He didn't have a beginning. He *is* the beginning!

Nothing created God. He is *uncreated.* He didn't get his life from another source. Life is *in him.* It always has been, and it always will be.

John goes on to say that God created everything and gave life to it. God made everything we see and enjoy. He created our world. He created outer space—the sun, the planets, and the stars. He created each one of us. Every breath we take is a gift from him.

---

* John was born in AD 6 and lived for nearly one hundred years. He is commonly referred to as "the disciple Jesus loved." He was the only disciple present at Calvary when Jesus was crucified. He authored the Gospel of John, 1 John, 2 John, 3 John, and Revelation—all New Testament Bible books.

Everything exists because God—who is the source of life—created it and is now sustaining it.

Death is an intruder in God's creation. Death is an enemy to God, because he is the source of life. God created us for life, not death, and he doesn't want any of us to die. In Ezekiel 33, he begs us to choose life: "As surely as I live, I do not want any who are wicked to die. I want them to stop doing evil and live. Stop! Stop your wicked ways! You don't want to die, do you?"[5]

At first, this Bible passage doesn't seem to make much sense. God says he doesn't want us to die, but we know from experience that every person on this planet is going to die someday. Also, God implies here that doing evil is what leads to death. But we know from experience that, often, "the good die young." Innocent children die all the time. And we know very well that we will also die, regardless of whether we are "good" or "evil."

On the surface, it doesn't quite add up. But God is trying to help us understand that *life and death aren't really about whether we're breathing or not.* True life is not about oxygen. True death is not about the lack of oxygen. There is a difference between existing and living. We are obsessed with existing, but God wants us to *live.*

Just because we're breathing doesn't mean we're *alive.* That's what Jesus was trying to explain when he said he had come to give us life! (Jesus was talking to people who were breathing.) God is eager to give this life—eternal life—to anyone who wants it. He wants us to accept this gift and live with him forever.

The apostle Paul† described it this way: "This body that can be destroyed must clothe itself with something that can never be destroyed. And this body that dies must clothe itself with something that can never die."[6]

Paul says God's gift of eternal life is like a jacket. He pictures us "putting on" this immortality in the same way that we put on a jacket when we're going out. We, who can die, will clothe ourselves with God, who cannot die. We, who are mortal, will clothe ourselves with God, who is immortal. We don't become immortal. God, in his generosity, shares *his* immortality with us.

Life is not a thing. Life is a person. God *is life*, but he shares that life with us. Until that day comes, though, Paul says that our life in God is guaranteed—even if we stop breathing. He said, "Whether we're awake with the living or asleep with the dead, we're alive with [Christ]."[7]

---

† The apostle Paul was the most notable of the early Christian missionaries. Born Saul of Tarsus, he was a high-ranking Jewish leader until he underwent a dramatic conversion on the road to Damascus. Paul wrote much of the New Testament, and scholars regard his writings as the earliest-written books of the New Testament. Having reached out to both Jews and Gentiles with the gospel message, he spent two years under arrest in Rome before being beheaded.

At first, it may seem strange that we could be "dead" and "alive" at the same time. But Paul refers to "dying" on this planet as going to sleep. Jesus also referred to it that way when his friend Lazarus died.‡

That means true life isn't measured by our breathing. And true death isn't measured by our *not* breathing. The "death" we experience on this planet is not true death. It's just a period of sleep that we're all going to wake up from. (We call this the "first death.")

God isn't concerned about this "death." Our going to sleep is not a problem for him, because he can undo it. He has the power to wake us all up. But there is a death that God can't undo.[8] (We call this the "second death.") This is real death, the death he is trying to keep us from.

That's the meaning of God's plea in Ezekiel 33. God is warning us that if we embrace sin, it will disconnect us from him. We can't live without that connection, because God is the only source of life in the universe. He doesn't want us to hold on to anything that would make us refuse his gift of life.

But is that really how it works? Does sin make us run away from life? We can see a vivid example of this in a story about the

---

‡ You can read that amazing story in John, chapter 11.

Israelites§ and their leader Moses.** As the head of the Israelite nation, Moses repeatedly tried to draw the people into a closer relationship with God. Moses was one of God's friends. He knew God, and he trusted God. The Bible says that God "would speak to Moses face to face, as a man speaks with his friend."[9]

On one of those occasions, Moses returned home after speaking personally with God. When he entered the camp, the Israelites reacted in a very strange way: "When Moses came down from Mount Sinai, he had spoken with the Lord. When Aaron and all the Israelites saw Moses, his face was radiant, and *they were afraid* to come near him."[10]

Moses's face was radiant with God's glory, and that frightened the people. Instead of being drawn to God's glory, the Israelites were terrified. That's what happens when we embrace sin. Sin can't stand to be in God's wonderful, life-filled presence. (Some say that God can't tolerate being in the presence of evil, but it's really the other way around. Evil can't tolerate being in God's presence.) God doesn't reject sinners. Sinners reject God.

---

§ The Israelites were descendents of the Biblical patriarch Jacob (who later became known as "Israel"). The nation was divided into twelve tribes, one tribe for each of Jacob's twelve sons. Much of the Old Testament is about how God interacted with the Israelites, his chosen people.

** Moses, a Hebrew born in Egypt around 1391 BC, became the leader of the Israelites. Under God's command, he led them out of slavery in Egypt to the Promised Land. He talked with God on Mount Sinai and delivered the Ten Commandments, which God wrote with his finger on tablets of stone. Moses also authored the first five books of the Bible, commonly referred to as the Torah.

This is why God said that evil leads to true death. If we embrace evil, we will continually hide from God. We will eventually reject him completely and refuse his gift of eternal life. Breaking that connection with him will result in true death, a sleep we can't wake up from. This is why God pleads with us: "Turn your backs on your rebellious living so that sin won't drag you down. Clean house. No more rebellions, please. Get a new heart! Get a new spirit! Why would you choose to die?"[11]

In God's creation, death—*real* death—is an enemy. God is all about life, and he wants us to live with him forever. Life is found *only* in him, but he came so we could have life, too. And have it to the full.

Reality show

God's honesty

A lie has speed, but truth has endurance.
—*Edgar J. Mohn*

When God says something, should we believe him? Does he tell the truth, or does he lie? Can we really trust what he says? How can we know for sure?

After visiting the Tree of the Knowledge of Good and Evil, Adam and Eve grappled with these questions. In their newly created state, they weren't really prepared to handle such questions. Overwhelmed and confused, they made costly mistakes that quickly unraveled their happy paradise.

Before that encounter, God had warned them to stay away from this tree. He said eating its fruit would kill them.[1] The Bible doesn't say whether Adam and Eve questioned God about this strange "rule." Perhaps, at first, they weren't even curious.

However, not long into the story, we can see why God warned them about the tree. God created this planet in the midst of a war. And at the Tree of the Knowledge of Good and Evil, Satan was planning to bring the war to our planet. He planned to tempt God's newest creatures to join him in his rebellion.

God's enemy was at the tree! If Adam and Eve had stayed away from it, they would have escaped Satan's temptation. They wouldn't have encountered those difficult questions. They wouldn't have placed themselves in a situation they weren't prepared to handle.

They could only be tempted by Satan at that tree. The fact that Adam and Eve didn't encounter him anywhere else in the garden suggests that God had restricted him to the tree. God allowed him access to the garden, but not unlimited access. He couldn't follow Adam and Eve around, pestering them with endless temptation. God confined him to the tree and then warned Adam and Eve not to go near it.

Unfortunately, Eve got curious one day. She wandered by the tree and saw a serpent curled up in its branches. All of a sudden, the serpent talked to her! Eve didn't realize it, but the serpent was really Satan, God's enemy, in disguise.[2]

Satan engaged Eve in a conversation about the tree. He asked her if God had really told them not to eat its fruit. Eve replied that, yes, God had told them it would kill them. But Satan said, "You will not certainly die…For God knows that when you eat of it your eyes will be opened, and you will be like God, knowing good and evil."[3]

All of a sudden, "eating the fruit" took on a whole new dimension. With our 20/20 hindsight, we can see that this wasn't a simple matter of digesting some food. No, it quickly became something more subtle and sinister. After the serpent claimed that God was selfishly withholding this fruit from her, Eve had to make a choice. Was she going to believe the serpent? Was she going to allow herself to be "held down" by God? After such accusations, if Eve ate the fruit, it would prove that she *agreed with the serpent.*

On the surface, it may seem like the serpent hadn't really said anything too awful about God. That's precisely why God warned Adam and Eve to stay away from the tree. Satan is a master of deception, and there was no way they could match wits with him. Eve found that out the hard way. It didn't take too long for Satan to artfully throw down some heavy accusations about God.

You will not certainly die. In her first response to Satan, Eve said that God had warned them not to eat from the tree, or they would die. Satan immediately contradicted that by saying, "You will not certainly die." In other words, he said, "God is a liar. You can't trust him. Just because he tells you something doesn't mean it's true."

Right off the bat, Satan went for the jugular. A good relationship can only be built on trust. If you don't trust someone, you won't be willing to relate to that person in a real and personal way. You may be nervous or "on your guard" all the time. This is why Satan raised the issue of trust. He knew if he could get us to distrust God, it would automatically damage our relationship.

God knows that when you eat of it your eyes will be opened. Satan followed up the accusation that God is a liar with a worse accusation—God is a selfish, power-hungry dictator. The implication here was that God lies in order to hold us down.

Satan claimed that God was afraid of losing his control over the universe. To avoid that, Satan said, God would stoop to any means necessary to secure his position.

You will be like God. There is a double lie in this statement—a double lie in just five words! First, Satan implied that God lies to us because he's afraid of competition. Satan claimed God knew that if Adam and Eve ate the fruit, they would also become gods, and God didn't want that to happen. To avoid that, Satan said, God lied to them and tried to frighten them into staying away from the tree.

A little farther under the surface, the second lie in this statement was that created beings can become gods. In heaven, Satan rebelled because he wanted to be a god. He suggested to Eve that she could experience the same thing.

Of course, this is utter nonsense. Being *uncreated* is one of the qualities that makes God who he is. There is no way a *created* being can become an *uncreated* being. Once you're *created,* you're *created.*

But it worked. Eve ate the fruit.

Satan's lies appeared convincing. In fact, at first it seemed he was actually telling the truth: God had told Adam and Eve that eating the fruit would kill them. However, after they ate the fruit, they *didn't* die. They were forced to leave their garden paradise and deal with the consequences of their sin, but they didn't die.

That must have been confusing. It must have seemed that God had been lying all along. How could he prove he had really been telling the truth? How could he convince us that he wasn't a liar? How could he prove that sin really does lead to death?

The answer seems almost too simple: he showed us. He came to our planet himself to live and die—*really* die—so we would know the truth.

God may have looked like a liar after Adam and Eve ate the fruit, but the death of Jesus changed that.* As Paul explained in his letter to the Romans, Jesus came here to die so we could know that God tells the truth. He did this because, for centuries, he allowed sin to continue so we could see where it would really lead. Jesus died to show that God told the truth about sin and death.[4]

Jesus was nailed to a cross, but he didn't actually die from being crucified. His death was not like any other "death" that had ever happened on this planet. It was different. It was *real* death.

Jesus died as a result of being fully separated from God.[5] In fact, he began to die in the Garden of Gethsemane,[6] long before he was beaten and nailed to the cross.

The cross was an object lesson. It was a self-demonstration of *real* death. Jesus's death proved that God wasn't a liar. On the cross, God showed us what he meant when he said, "If you ever eat fruit from that tree, you will die!"[7] God sacrificed himself so we would know what death is and what causes it.

This sort of self-demonstration was famously undertaken by Dr. Evan O'Neill Kane, the modern pioneer of local anesthesia. For

---

* Jesus was crucified on a cross at Calvary. This was the most common form of execution in the Roman Empire. But Jesus didn't die from being crucified. Instead, he died as a result of being fully separated from God in a demonstration of the "second" death.

many years, he had argued that general anesthesia for minor surgery was risky and unnecessary. Instead, he advocated local anesthesia.

The idea of local anesthesia was attractive to other doctors, but they weren't convinced it would be 100% effective. They were afraid local anesthesia could wear off in the middle of surgery, which would be excruciating for their patients. In addition, most patients didn't like the idea of being awake during surgery.

Dr. Kane, however, knew he was right. So, he set out to change the minds of his medical colleagues. Ignoring all the objections, he successfully performed the world's first surgery using local anesthesia. And since he couldn't find a willing patient, *he performed the surgery on himself.* The doctor became the patient![8]

That's precisely what God did to show us what happens when we separate ourselves from him—he performed the separation on himself! On the cross, Jesus died from being totally separated from God. This is why he cried, "My God, my God, why have you abandoned me?"[9]

Jesus died this way to show us how sin causes death. The Bible says that Jesus "became sin" for us.[10] In other words, he demonstrated that sin kills us by completely separating us from God. By observing his death, we learn two important things: first, sin *really does* lead to death; second, God *does not* cause that death. It is a natural result of separating ourselves from him.

Because of Jesus's life, we know the truth about God. Because of Jesus's death, we know the truth about sin. But this self-demonstration of the truth wasn't an isolated event: God's very existence is truth. This is why Jesus said, "I am the truth."[11] God doesn't just *know* the truth or even just *tell* the truth. *He is the truth!*

In the Garden of Eden, Satan told Eve that God would lie to us in order to keep us down. But in the Garden of Gethsemane, Jesus proved that he would show us the truth at any cost in order to lift us up. He is the original reality show.

Higher power

God's omnipotence

*Nearly all men can stand adversity, but if you want to test
a man's character, give him power.*
—*Abraham Lincoln*

God is sheer power. He is a self-contained, unlimited power supply. The Bible describes him as the one who breathes out stars,[1] the one who contains the ocean with invisible reins,[2] the one who commands the sun to stand still,[3] and the one who makes wine out of water.[4] God is not bound or limited by anyone or anything. His power is stamped all over history. From mighty planets to newborn babies, everything is autographed with his might.

Power to Create

The Bible says that God can create *ex nihilo,* which means "from nothing." An old joke goes like this: A group of scientists decides to find God so they can tell him to get lost. They say they no longer need him since they have discovered how to create life. God listens patiently to them, smiling. Then, he challenges the scientists to a man-creating contest, with the stipulation that they must create from dirt, as he did in the beginning. They agree. Eagerly, one of them bends down to scoop up some dirt. And God chuckles and says, "No, friend. Get your own dirt."

God doesn't even need dirt to get started! In the book of Psalms, David* says that God speaks and things materialize: "By the word of the Lord were the heavens made, their starry host by the breath of his mouth. For he spoke, and it came to be; he commanded, and it stood firm."[5] The sun in our solar system is a star, and it's not even a particularly big star (as stars go). Yet, David describes God as being the one who breathed out the stars. Can you imagine that? God opened his mouth, and the sun came out. That's incredible!

Power Over Nature

God has full control over nature. After the Israelites had been slaves in Egypt for hundreds of years, God decided it was high time to free them.

---

* David was the second king of Israel and is described in the Bible as a man after God's own heart. He was an acclaimed warrior, musician, and poet. He authored many of the songs found in Psalms, an Old Testament Bible book.

During this dramatic rescue process, God tried to get Pharaoh's† attention through some incredible displays of power. One by one, ten plagues fell on Egypt. Among them were swarms of flies, a tidal wave of frogs, and a plague of darkness. He even turned the water in the Nile River to blood—and then back to water. Curiously, none of these plagues affected the part of the land where the Israelites lived.

Eventually, Pharaoh released the Israelites. But soon after they left, Pharaoh changed his mind and went after them. The whole nation was trapped. With the Red Sea on one side and the Egyptian army on the other side in hot pursuit, there was nowhere to go.

That's when God split the Red Sea into two huge walls of water so the people could walk across to safety on dry ground.‡ Just as soon as the last Israelite foot left the sea floor, the walls of water came crashing down.

It would be difficult to deny God's power. It's obvious that he has the power to do whatever he wants, whenever he wants. No-

---

† The most powerful person in ancient Egypt was the pharaoh. The pharaoh was the political and religious leader of the Egyptian people. He owned all the land, made laws, collected taxes, defended Egypt against foreigners, and represented the gods.

‡ Read the whole story in Exodus, chapters 7-14.

body can stop him. Nobody can oppose him. Should that make us nervous? Perhaps.

On this planet, kingdoms and governments are constantly engaged in a struggle for power. Either they try to gain more power for themselves, or they try to keep other nations from acquiring more power than they have. What's the real issue in this struggle? Is it the power, or is it the fear of how the power of others will be used?

Power is always used (or abused) according to a person's character. Imagine Adolf Hitler with unlimited power. That's a frightening thought! During World War II, the world saw how Hitler used power. Even with *limited* power, he was unbelievably cruel and sadistic. Imagine if he had been able to do whatever he wanted, whenever he wanted!

On the other hand, imagine Mother Theresa with unlimited power. Even with absolutely *no* power, she changed lives and inspired the world. Imagine if she had been able to do whatever she wanted, whenever she wanted!

What's the difference between Adolf Hitler and Mother Theresa? Character. Character always guides the use of power. So, if God's character was questionable, we might be very nervous about his unlimited power. We might live in fear, never knowing what would happen next. We could be in for some major problems. Fortunately, God has proved that he is not a Hitler.

God's immense power puts a spotlight on his character. The way he uses his power tells us a lot about the kind of person he is. God is all-powerful, for sure, but he doesn't flaunt that power. In fact, *he doesn't even use his power to benefit himself.* Instead, he uses it *to benefit us.*

Paul once wrote that God's strength is made perfect in our weakness.[6] We have no power in ourselves, but God shares his power with us and teaches us to use it as he does. As we draw closer to God, we become the kind of people *who can be trusted with power.*

As we remain in friendship with God, he continually gives more and more of his power to us. This means that we are already enabled to do whatever God asks us to do—*because of him!* He provides all the power we need. That's why Paul, who was well aware of his weaknesses, said, "I can do all things through Christ, because he gives me strength."[7]

As we receive God's power and learn to use it as he does, we also become more like him. Receiving his power restores his character in us. That's because God's character and his power are undeniably linked. When it comes to God, his character doesn't just guide the use of his power, his character *is* his power. That's why he is the most powerful being in the universe!

Heads or tails

God's humility

True humility is contentment.
—*Henri Frederic Amiel*

Imagine the Creator of the Universe as a man, kneeling in the dust. It's the same dust he used centuries before to mold the first man. He breathed into that dust, and it came alive.

Now, he kneels in the dust again, dirty and tired and hungry. With a towel around his waist and a bowl of water next to him, he is washing dirty feet.

He washes the dirt and grime off the feet of his disciples before their last meal together. Normally, a servant would handle such an unsavory task. But there is no servant on hand. So Jesus, the one who created these men, kneels down to do a slave's job.*

_____

* You can read the story in John, chapter 13.

The Creator of the Universe doing the work of a servant? That's outrageous! What earthly king in his right mind would go out and feed the pigs? What dictator would put in a hard day's work so one of his subjects could take a day off? What leader of a nation would roll up his sleeves and clean toilets for a day? What ruler in his right mind does that? God.

Even if God had come to this planet as a superstar or a king, the transformation from Supreme Being to human being alone would have been immensely humbling. Think about it: the Creator of the Universe became a human. The God who breathes out stars became a speck. (Creator turned *created*—now *that's* humility!) We can't begin to comprehend how *small* he became.

At the very least, he should have lived the most luxurious life this planet could afford. But he didn't. Instead, the description of his life given by Isaiah is heart wrenching:

> He was hated and rejected by people.
>> He had much pain and suffering.
> People would not even look at him.
>> He was hated, and we didn't even notice
>> him.
>
> But he took our suffering on him
>> and felt our pain for us.
> We saw his suffering
>> and *thought God was punishing him.*

He was beaten down and punished,
> but he didn't say a word.

He was like a lamb being led to be killed.
> He was quiet, as a sheep is quiet while its
> wool is being cut; he never opened his
> mouth.

Men took him away roughly and unfairly.
> He died without children to continue his
> family.

He was put to death;
> he was punished for the sins of my
> people.[1]

The Creator of the Universe came to our planet so we could get to know him. He didn't demand anything from anyone. He didn't insist that anyone submit to his authority. He didn't put his incredible power on display in an effort to coerce people into following him.

On the contrary, people flocked to Jesus because of his character. He was a pleasant person to be with. He spoke plainly about God. He encouraged people and gave them hope. He healed people from horrible, disfiguring diseases. He never condemned anyone who came to him. He was gentle, kind, and sincere.

Underneath this tenderness, however, was immense power. Jesus had complete control over nature.[2] He had complete control over life and death.³ When he was falsely arrested, he had the power to escape.⁴ When one of his disciples cut off the ear of an enemy soldier, Jesus picked it up and instantly reattached it.⁵ He could have done whatever he wanted, whenever he wanted. Yet, the Creator of the Universe chose to submit to painful torture at the hands of his own creatures.

It's almost unbelievable that such a powerful God could be so humble. In a world where we normally associate power with arrogance, humility doesn't seem to fit. But God's immense power doesn't make him distant or unfriendly. In fact, sometimes we can lose sight of God's powerful position because—as Jesus said—God prefers that we be his friends instead of his servants.⁶

From our frame of reference, this seems absurd. What king prefers friends to servants? After all, the whole point of being a king is so you can have servants.

For God, however, the whole point of being a king is so he can *be a servant*. His power doesn't place him beyond our reach or make him unable or unwilling to serve. He's not so big and grand that he can't come down to our level and meet us where we are. On the contrary, service and humility are the *keys to greatness* in his kingdom.

Jesus was trying to teach his disciples about that kind of greatness as he washed their feet. Not long before that last meal together, the disciples had been arguing about which of them would be the greatest in God's kingdom.[7]

Since Jesus knew what they had been discussing, he decided to show them exactly how to achieve greatness. So, he knelt down and did the servant's job. He even washed the feet of his betrayer.

At first, this seems backward, doesn't it? We commonly associate power with the use of force, so using power to assert authority seems very natural to us. However, the truth is that power is most convincing when it is expressed in humility and restraint.

In the film *Schindler's List*, Amon Goeth, a German commandant, has this exchange with Oskar Schindler about having power over the Jews:

GOETH: Control is power. That's power.

SCHINDLER: Is that why they fear us?

GOETH: We have the power to kill; that's why they fear us.

SCHINDLER: They fear us because we have the power to kill arbitrarily...That's not power, though...Power is when we have every justification to kill— and we don't.

GOETH: You think that's power?

SCHINDLER: That's what the emperor said. A

     man steals something; he's brought

     in before the emperor; he throws

     himself down on the ground; he begs

     for mercy; he knows he's going to

     die. And the emperor...pardons him.

     This worthless man, he lets him go.

     That's power, Amon. That is power.[8]

True power is displayed most forcefully in humility. Jesus said, "Whoever is your servant is the greatest among you. Whoever makes himself great will be made humble. Whoever makes himself humble will be made great."[9]

This isn't true because God suggested it. It's true because it's a law of life, and God personifies it. The way he exercises his power is *precisely* what makes him so powerful. Though he is infinite in majesty and power, our God became the servant of all. The Creator became the servant of the *created!*

Because he has humbled himself in this way, he will be honored above everything else forever. Once again, God proves that he tells the truth: humility *really does* lead to greatness. Though he does not exalt himself, those who love and admire God will worship him throughout eternity. In his letter to the Philippians, Paul describes in detail how it works:

> In your lives you must think and act like Christ Jesus. Christ himself was like God in everything. But he did not think that being equal with God was something to be used for his own benefit. But he gave up his place with God and made himself nothing. He was born as a man and became like a servant. And when he was living as a man, he humbled himself and was fully obedient to God, even when that caused his death—death on a cross.

> So God raised him to the highest place. God made his name greater than every other name so that every knee will bow to the name of Jesus—everyone in heaven, on earth, and under the earth. And everyone will confess that Jesus Christ is Lord and bring glory to God the Father.[10]

Once upon a time, the Supreme Ruler of the Universe came to our planet. Not as a superstar, but as a servant.

That's power, Amon. That is power.

O holy knight

God's holiness

Holy is the way God is.
To be holy, he does not conform to a standard; he is that standard.
—*AW Tozer*

In modern culture, the word *holy* often has a spiritual connotation. It is commonly used to mean "pious" or "devout." The original meaning of the word, however, was this: "having the quality of total otherness." The word *holy* describes something that is totally *other than* what we know. It describes something that is set apart, in a category all its own.

God is holy. That means there is no being in the universe like him. God exists in his own special category. Nothing else compares to him or even comes close. He's the only one who is immortal.[1] He's the only source of life.[2] He's the only one who can create a universe from nothing.[3] He is not dependent on anything or anyone for survival. He is completely and utterly self-contained. He is flaw-less and perfect. Self-sufficient. Autonomous. Holy.

What about us, then? Should we be holy? *Can* we be holy? There are many Christian songs that deal with the idea of becoming holy. There's even an old hymn titled *Take Time to be Holy*. But if being holy means being self-sufficient and not dependent on any-thing else for life, how *can* we be holy? As creatures, we are *utterly dependent* on God for life. We can't exist without him. We can't be-come self-sufficient.

If this is true, if we can't become *holy* on our own, where does that leave us? Are we destined to remain *unholy?* From a Bibli-cal standpoint, that doesn't seem desirable. The Bible says that what is *unholy* can't stand to be in the presence of what is *holy*.[4] What are we to do?

Isaiah must have been concerned about this. In his book, he wrote about an interesting vision he had. Consider his experience:

> It was in the year King Uzziah died that I saw
> the Lord. He was sitting on a lofty throne, and
> the train of his robe filled the Temple. At-
> tending him were mighty seraphim, each hav-
> ing six wings. With two wings they covered
> their faces, with two they covered their feet,
> and with two they flew. They were calling out
> to each other,

"Holy, holy, holy is the Lord of Heaven's Armies! The whole earth is filled with his glory!"

Their voices shook the Temple to its foundations, and the entire building was filled with smoke.

Then I said, "It's all over! I am doomed, for I am a sinful man. I have filthy lips, and I live among a people with filthy lips. Yet I have seen the King, the Lord of Heaven's Armies."

Then one of the seraphim flew to me with a burning coal he had taken from the altar with a pair of tongs. He touched my lips with it and said, "See, this coal has touched your lips. Now your guilt is removed, and your sins are forgiven."[5]

Here, we see how God's holiness interacts with us. *His holiness makes things pure.* It takes unclean things and makes them clean. His holiness encounters our guilt and removes it, leaving us feeling refreshed and renewed. When we approach God, he shares his holiness with us. In his presence, our unholiness is transformed.

We can't ever become holy like God is. We can't enter that set-apart, "totally other" category he's in. He is the creator, and we are the created. That's how it will always be. But when we come close to him in relationship, God freely shares his holiness with us. Just as we "put on" his immortality, so we can "put on" his holiness.

Though we can't enter the category of "total otherness" that God is in, his holiness "sets us apart" in a special way. We are created in his image.[6] This means he created us to be *individuals*. He gave us the ability to think and the power to make choices. God wants us to exercise these abilities, especially the power to think. He doesn't want us to be mere reflectors of the culture around us.

Incredible, isn't it? God prefers that we think for ourselves. In fact, he doesn't even want us to merely reflect his own thoughts! If he did, he could just tell us what to believe, or he could have made us as robots. Instead, he asks us to "come and reason" with him.[7] He gives us evidence to consider so we can make our own decisions. As we are touched by his holiness, his image is restored in us, and we become true thinkers.

So what happens if we refuse God's holiness? A little later in Isaiah's vision, God told him to return to the people with this warning: "You will listen and listen, but you will not understand. You will look and look, but you will not learn."[8] God goes on to say that if these people continue to reject him, they will end up with dull minds, blind eyes, and deaf ears. All of them.

When we reject God and his holiness, we end up like re-tarded sheep: deaf, blind, and mute. God's warning to the Israelites was that, without him, they would become a bunch of conformist numbskulls, unable to think for themselves. They would lose their individuality and their power to think and act.

When God's holiness touches us, we become more unified with those around us, but we don't become *uniform*. God's holiness produces unity, *not uniformity*. As our relationship with God deepens, our individuality actually expresses itself *more,* not less. God doesn't want an entire race of lookalike robots. He enjoys outrageous vari-ety.* That's why he created so many different kinds of people, plants, and animals.

The closer we come to God, the more we can truly be our-selves. He has created each of us unique and has given us special talents. Without him, however, our individuality gradually erodes as we blindly conform to every passing fad.

God delights in giving us the gift of his holiness, because it helps us discover who we really are—who he created us to be. As our holy knight, he rescues us from the inevitable drudgery of a life lived in conformity without him.

---

* Have you ever seen a duck-billed platypus?

The Deity is in the details

God's orderliness

There is an orderliness in the universe; there is an unalterable law governing everything and every being that exists or lives. It is no blind law, for no blind law can govern the conduct of living beings.
—Mahatma Ghandi

Have you ever watched a documentary on the way a baby—an entire person—develops from two single cells? Have you ever marveled over the tiny fingers and toes of a newborn?

If so, you have probably reveled in the thought, as David did, of how fearfully and wonderfully we are made.[1] Our bodies are intricately detailed and organized. Each system functions in harmony with every other system. God designed us that way.

Paul tried to explain this in his letter to the people who lived in Corinth:

> Yes, the body has many different parts, not just one part. If the foot says, "I am not a part of the body because I am not a hand," that does not make it any less a part of the body. And if the ear says, "I am not part of the body because I am not an eye," would that make it any less a part of the body?
>
> If the whole body were an eye, how would you hear? Or if your whole body were an ear, how would you smell anything?
>
> But our bodies have many parts, and God has put each part just where he wants it. How strange a body would be if it had only one part! Yes, there are many parts, but only one body.[2]

This is how God works. He is orderly and purposeful. He creates in an intricate way, paying attention to every last detail. He doesn't create stand-alone entities. He makes intricately woven environments (such as our bodies) where all the individual parts work together for the good of the whole.

God's orderliness is a reflection of his holiness, which produces *unity*, not *uniformity*. Think about the organs in your body. They are anything but *uniform*. The heart looks wildly different from the hand, and they both serve the body in completely different ways. The brain is nothing like the nose, and they both serve totally different functions in the body. Yet, all these different parts *unify* to form one body.

In God's orderly creation, all things are designed to exist in an other-centered process of give-and-take. We see this most clearly in nature.[3] The cycle of photosynthesis, for example, only works when there is *both* give and take. Contrary to the belief that "taking" is bad, every participant in the cycle has to take something. The key, though, is that the taking is for the purpose of giving.

Trees and plants take the carbon dioxide out of the atmosphere, but they take it to make oxygen. Animals and people take the oxygen, but they take it to make carbon dioxide. The trees and plants produce the oxygen necessary for the survival of the animals and people. And animals and people produce the carbon dioxide necessary for the survival of the trees and plants. So, the cycle of give-and-take ensures the survival of everything on this planet.

Imagine what would happen if the trees and plants decided that they were tired of giving. What if they decided to continue taking the carbon dioxide, but refused to make any more oxygen? Soon, without oxygen, the human race would die. This would stop the flow of carbon dioxide, and then all the trees and plants would die. If one group began taking without giving in return, *everything* would die, *including the ones who decided to stop giving.*

This cycle of give-and-take is also represented perfectly in the body. Every organ, every system, and every cell in your body takes from every other organ, system, and cell. But they take to give. We have a name for rogue, hoarding cells in the body. Cells that take but don't give are called cancer cells. This kind of *selfish taking* results in the *death of the whole body*, including the cancer cells.

This orderliness we see all around us is no accident. It's no coincidence that nature is designed to work according to the law of give-and-take. Nature is orderly because the God who created it is orderly. He creates based on the law of give-and-take because he embodies it.

In Jesus, we see the ultimate example of give-and-take. While he was on this planet, Jesus took everything he needed from his Father. All his power, his compassion, and his peace came straight from heaven. This wasn't selfish taking, however. He took *to give*. He took all that power, compassion, and peace from his Father and poured it out into the lives of everyone who met him. Jesus was an open channel of blessing to everyone he encountered.

We have the same opportunity as we draw closer to God. The more we come to know and understand God, the more he gives us. God gives and gives and gives, but he can't force it into us. We must be willing to *take* it. We can't refuse to take because we think taking is selfish. If we refuse to take, we will remain *empty*— just like a balloon that refuses to be blown up with air.

But God intends for us to take *in order to give.* He doesn't want us to selfishly hang on to his gifts, clutching at them like we're desperate. We must be willing to give. If we refuse to give, we will become *bloated*—just like a balloon that is blown up with too much air. There is nowhere for the air to go, and the balloon is in danger of popping!

However, when we are open to both taking *and* giving, we become like Jesus. When we are willing to take and give, we are an open channel of God's blessing, flooding the lives of those around us with his goodness. God desperately wants to bless us. You can bet that when he recognizes an open channel, he will pour in the blessings like a tsunami!

God designed things to work in this orderly way so the needs of all his creatures would be met. God is certainly the source of all blessing, but he invites us to work with him. He gives us the opportunity to meet the needs of others with the blessings he provides. Through the process of give-and-take, we all get in on the business of life and love. When we take from him to serve others, the Source of All is praised and glorified.

And the circuit of blessings continues.

What's love got to do with it?

God's love

We could all wish to be preceded in this world by a love story.
—*Don Schneider*

In his song *The Other Side of Me*, Michael W. Smith marries love and mathematics: "If love were mathematical, you'd understand the sum to the heart's equation where one and one makes one. And lonely equals me minus you."[1]

How about slipping an axiom in there from high school geometry? Do you remember this one?

$$If\ a = b,\ and\ b = c,\ then\ a = c$$

Could this axiom be applied to God's love?

After spending three years with Jesus, John wrote this: "Dear friends, we should love each other, because love comes from

God. Everyone who loves has become God's child and knows God. Whoever does not love does not know God, because God is love."[2]

God's love goes beyond acting to *being*. God doesn't just act lovingly; he *is* love. If we see him, we see love personified. Let's put this together with Paul's famous statements about love in 1 Corinthians 13:1-7. For instance, Paul says that love is patient. By applying the axiom, we arrive at this conclusion:

If God is love, and love is patient, then God is patient.

What would the entire passage look like if we applied the axiom and replaced the word *love* with *God* ?

> I may speak in different languages of people or even angels. But if I do not [know God], I am only a noisy bell or a crashing cymbal. I may have the gift of prophecy. I may understand all the secret things of God and have all knowledge, and I may have faith so great I can move mountains. But even with all these things, if I do not [know God], then I am nothing. I may give away everything I have, and I may even give my body as an offering to be burned. But I gain nothing if I do not [know God].
>
> [God] is patient and kind. [God] is not jealous, does not brag, and is not proud. [God] is not rude, is not selfish, and does not get upset with others. [God] does not count up

wrongs that have been done. [God] takes no
pleasure in evil but rejoices over the truth.
[God] patiently accepts all things. [God] always trusts, always hopes, and always en-
dures.[3]

Isn't this a beautiful picture of God? At first glance, this may
seem too good to be true. This is certainly a different picture of
God than the one sometimes presented by the world. But the Bible
plainly states that God is love, and if he is love, then he is love in all
its aspects.

God is patient and kind. By nature, God is caring. He cares about all
his creatures—even those who choose to reject him. He never
needs to be manipulated or persuaded to care about us. One hall-
mark of the false gods in the Bible was that their "subjects" often
had to find ways to appease them. They would cut themselves, ex-
ploit others, and even kill their own children to manipulate their
gods.

We don't have to do anything like that to get the attention
of the true God. On the contrary, he's the one who takes the initia-
tive in our relationship. He is always seeking us out. He doesn't wait
for us to come to him. He comes to us. He is infinitely patient and
kind with all his children.

God does not count up wrongs that have been done. As a lifelong Christian, I've heard repeatedly that we should understand that we don't "merit" God's favor. I've heard that not only do we need to understand this, but we also need to let God know that we understand this. It's apparently important for us to know that we don't deserve his love and attention. Is this really true? No!

The truth is that if God is love, he doesn't keep a record of wrongs to hold over our heads. He *never* tells us that we're unworthy. And even when *we* try to tell him that we believe we're unworthy, he doesn't listen.[4] He scoops us up and welcomes us with open arms. Regardless of what we've done or how long we've been away from him, he eagerly accepts us.

God loves us for the same reason a parent loves a child—because he created us. We are his. Trying to decide whether we "merit" his love completely misses the point. God isn't concerned about merit or worth. His love doesn't *require* worth from us. His love *bestows* worth on us!

God doesn't love us because we decide to be his children. We are his children *because* he loves us! So, do I merit God's love? *Absolutely!* And so do you. God's love *crowns us* with merit. Our worth comes from God and the fact that he showers all of us with love.

Love is the great bridge between God's personal and relational character traits. Everything he does is motivated by love.

Love drives God's internal activity. That means the Father, Son, and Spirit always relate to one another in love. As Don Schneider once said, we could all wish to be preceded in this world by a love story. Because of what we know about God, we know that this wish is a reality. *All of us* are preceded in this world by a love story. In fact, we are here because of the intense love that exists in the Trinity. That love expressed itself in our creation.

Love also empowers God's external activity. That means that God's primary motivation in creation and in his dealings with us is love. John recognized this, and that's why he wrote, "For God so loved the world that he gave his one and only Son, that whoever believes in him shall not perish but have eternal life."[5]

Love comes first. Love *always* comes first. Everything God does is driven by the fact that he "so loved." And John says this love eventually leads to eternal life. God loved, so he gave. Because he gave, we have the opportunity to choose life.

Without love, there is no life. But with love, life lasts forever. That's why Paul ended his famous passage on love by saying that love would never die.[6] We have been preceded in this world by a love story. And God wants to continue that love story with us for eternity.

Outer Beauty

God's external characteristics

God's character includes his external qualities.

These relational traits define the way God deals with his created beings.

God doesn't "decide" to be this way.

These traits are natural extensions of his inherent, internal qualities.

Thus, these qualities are eternal and unchanging.

Man's best friend

God's friendship

The best way to destroy an enemy is to make him a friend.
—Abraham Lincoln

Should we relate to God as servants or friends? Would one be better than the other, or are they equal choices? John recorded what Jesus's preference was: "I no longer call you slaves, because a master doesn't confide in his slaves. Now you are my friends, since I have told you everything the Father told me."[1]

In his rather stunning statement, Jesus says he wants us to be his friends. Not only does God prefer to serve instead of being served, but he prefers to have friends instead of subordinates. God desires friends because he wants to have a certain quality of relationship with us. A master doesn't confide in his slaves, and a slave doesn't dare question his master. But a friend is different.

A friend offers opinions. Abraham* was God's friend. One day, God came to his tent and sat down to a meal. Imagine fixing a meal for God in your home!

After they were done eating, God and Abraham walked down the road together. Their conversation is recorded in Genesis, chapter 18:

> The Lord said, "I have heard many complaints against the people of Sodom and Gomorrah. They are very evil. I will go down and see if they are as bad as I have heard. If not, I will know." So the men turned and went toward Sodom, but Abraham stood there before the Lord.
>
> Then Abraham approached him and asked, "Do you plan to destroy the good people along with the evil ones? What if there are fifty good people in that city? Will you still destroy it? Surely, you will save the city for the fifty good people living there. Surely you will not destroy the good people along with the evil ones; then they would be treated the same. You are the judge of all the earth. Won't you do what is right?"[2]

---

* Abraham, born around 2000 BC, is commonly regarded as the founding patriarch of Judaism. God made a special covenant with him and brought him to the land of Canaan. Abraham's son Isaac was conceived miraculously after his wife, Sarah, was past the childbearing age.

Abraham wanted to guard God's reputation. He knew what God was like, and he was concerned about anything that would tarnish God's good name. Abraham went on to bargain with God over the city, and God agreed that he would "spare the city" if there were ten good people living there. Now, God already knew there weren't ten good people in the city, but he didn't interrupt Abraham. He didn't say, "Trust me, Abe, you're wasting your time." That's because *engaging in friendship with us is more important to God than displaying his superiority.*

Moses was another close friend of God. He also wanted to guard God's reputation. When God told Moses that he was going to strike down the Israelites with a plague and, instead, make a great nation from Moses's descendants, this is how Moses replied: "Then the Egyptians will hear about it! By your power, you brought these people up from among them. If you put them to death all at one time, the nations who have heard this report about you will say, 'The Lord was not able to bring these people into the land he promised them on oath; so he slaughtered them in the desert.'"[3]

Moses flatly turned down God's offer to make him into a great nation. That is astonishing enough. But it's even more amazing that the reason Moses refused was because he wanted to protect God's reputation in the eyes of the surrounding heathen nations. That is a true sign of friendship.

A friend asks questions, even angry questions. Jonah† was a friend of God, even though he tried to run away from God when he received an assignment he didn't like. God had asked Jonah to go to Nineveh and warn the people to turn from their evil ways.

Jonah didn't want to go to Nineveh. The Ninevites were fierce enemies of the Israelites. Jonah didn't want to deliver God's message to them, because he knew how gracious and kind God was. Jonah didn't want God to be kind to his enemies!

After a whale of a detour,‡ Jonah went to Nineveh and delivered the message of impending doom. Afterward, he went to sit on a hill overlooking Nineveh. Much to Jonah's dismay, the Ninevites actually listened to him and repented. And God forgave them.

Jonah was furious: "He lost his temper. He yelled at God, 'God! I knew it—when I was back home, I knew this was going to happen! That's why I ran off to Tarshish! I knew you were sheer grace and mercy, not easily angered, rich in love, and ready at the drop of a hat to turn your plans of punishment into a program of forgiveness!'"[4]

---

† The prophet Jonah was born in Israel around 800 BC during the reign of King Jeroboam II. His story is told in the Old Testament Bible book of Jonah. He is famously known as the prophet who was swallowed by a whale after trying to run away from God.

‡ Read all about the big fish rescue in Jonah 1:15-17.

Far from wanting to guard God's reputation, Jonah was angry that God had actually lived up to his good name.§ He certainly wasn't bargaining for anyone's life. He would much rather have seen Nineveh go up in smoke.

Yet, it's interesting that Jonah was clearly taking advantage of God's gracious character—the very character he claimed to despise. He obviously knew that he could question God—even while he was furious—without being afraid.

Even in his anger, Jonah's behavior toward God was a testament to the truth about him: God prefers friends who *understand*, even when the process of understanding is fraught with intense emotion.

God didn't scold Jonah for his anger. Instead, God engaged him in conversation. It was hot in the desert, so God caused a plant to grow up over Jonah's head for shade. Then, God used the plant as an illustration to help Jonah understand how *he* felt about the Ninevites.

Isn't it incredible that the Creator of the Universe would act in such a loving, patient way? Instead of demanding a certain attitude or response from us, God takes us "as is." He works with us *where we are* to help us understand him better.

---

§ In his book *You, Jonah!*, author Thomas Carlisle depicts Jonah as lashing out against God with this strange insult: "You dirty Forgiver!"

A friend wants to understand, not just obey. As dependent, created beings, we should be willing to obey God. Being friends with him doesn't cancel the need for obedience. On the contrary, our friendship with God *enhances* our obedience.

God doesn't want the kind of obedience that comes from a servant. Make no mistake: he wants us to do what he asks, but he doesn't want us to do it *blindly.* He prefers that we understand *why* he is asking us to do something. Then, our obedience stems from the fact that we *agree* with the way God runs his universe.

This kind of obedience leads to salvation. When we are willing to listen, there isn't anything God can't accomplish. He can tell us, show us, or teach us anything we need to know. Author Graham Maxwell described this friendly attitude as "having enough confidence in God—based upon the *more-than-adequate evidence* revealed—to be willing to believe whatever he says, accept whatever he offers, and do whatever he wishes without reservation for the rest of eternity."[5]

This is salvation. It isn't a legal transaction. It's a friendship. God wants to live forever with friends. He is in the business of "getting rid of" his enemies—not by destroying them, but by helping them become his friends.

Giving it all he's got

God's giving

I have found that among its other benefits,
giving liberates the soul of the giver.
—*Maya Angelou*

By nature, God is a giver. The Bible is a long, historical account of the endless stream of God's gifts to humans. From Adam's first breath to the birth of Jesus, every moment of our planet's history is drenched in God's gifts.

The apostle James* put it this way: "Every desirable and beneficial gift comes out of heaven. The gifts are rivers of light cascading down from the Father of Light."[1] Put simply, God gives us everything we need.

---

* James was an apostle and influential leader in the early Christian church. He authored the New Testament book of James. At the time, there were several apostles with the name "James," so scholars dispute which one actually wrote the book. It is usually believed to be one of two: James, the son of Zebedee, or James, one of Jesus's half-brothers.

God takes care of our practical needs. He provides what we need for our daily lives. We don't have to worry about having enough or getting more. We don't have to pretend to be self-sufficient or think we have to fend for ourselves. Whatever we need, God has it and is willing to give it to us.

When God rescued the Israelites from slavery in Egypt, they had to travel through the desert to get to the land he had promised to give them. These people were on the run. They weren't prepared to take care of themselves in the desert. Their leader, Moses, must have been scared. He had millions of people in the desert with no food, water, or supplies. How would they survive?

God gave them water. When the people were thirsty, God instructed Moses to hit a rock with his stick. Moses did, and water gushed out of the rock.[2]

God gave them food. Every day, sweet bread fell from the sky.[3] The Israelites went out and gathered it fresh each morning—delicious bread they didn't even have to make!

In an environment of extreme temperatures, God made the Israelites comfortable. During the day, his presence was a cloud to shelter them from the harsh sun. During the night, when it became extremely cold, God's presence was a pillar of fire.[4]

Later in Israel's history, the prophet Elijah† was forced to go into hiding from an evil king. God led him to a brook where he could hide until it was safe. While Elijah relaxed by the water, God took care of all his needs by sending birds to feed him. "The ravens brought him bread and meat in the morning and meat in the evening, and he drank from the brook."[5]

No matter what circumstances we're in, God takes care of all our practical needs. He is able to provide for us anywhere, anytime, and in any way necessary for us to be taken care of. For a God who notices when a sparrow falls to the ground,[6] no need of ours is too small to escape his attention.

God takes care of our spiritual needs. From the moment sin infected our planet, human beings have struggled with guilt, fear, and remorse. These powerful emotions threaten to tear us away from God and destroy our relationship with him.

But God has just what we need to deal with these spiritual problems. He doesn't abandon us. In many ways throughout history, he has provided ways to lift us out of our guilt and shame.

---

† The prophet Elijah lived in the ninth century BC during the reigns of Ahab, Ahaziah, and Jehoram. He spent a great deal of time trying to draw the Israelites away from the foreign god Baal back to the true God. According to 2 Kings (an Old Testament Bible book), Elijah was taken up to heaven in a chariot of fire.

For example, Adam and Eve began to experience guilt and fear immediately after they ate "the forbidden fruit." The first thing they realized was that they were naked.[7] This made them feel vulnerable, awkward, and afraid. They tried to cover themselves up with some leaves and ran away to hide from God.

When God "found" them, he made clothes for them[8] so they wouldn't be ashamed of their nakedness. Right away, he made them feel comfortable.

Later in Earth's history, God devised a system of sacrifices for the Israelites.‡ This system was designed to deal with a person's guilt. First, God specified a sacrifice for every possible "sin" a person could commit. Nothing was overlooked. There were sacrifices for stealing, lying, and cheating. There were sacrifices for "intentional" and "unintentional" sins. God spelled it out in great detail.

Then, God instructed the Israelites to make these sacrifices at regular times or special times, when necessary. He assured them that by making these sacrifices, they would be forgiven.

By designing the sacrificial system, God was saying to the Israelites, "I'm not mad at you. Please bring your problems to me. I want to take care of them." By doing this, the Israelites were able to internalize God's forgiveness and acceptance.

‡ Read all about it in the book of Leviticus.

The sacrificial system was a brilliant way of turning an abstract concept, such as forgiveness, into a concrete reality. When an Israelite left the temple, he could know for sure that everything was right between him and God. This assurance removed the guilt and fear associated with coming to God in a sinful condition.

This system of sacrifices went on for centuries. After Jesus came, however, we didn't need to make sacrifices anymore. Through his life and death, Jesus made it clear that God freely forgives us. Understanding that he forgives us was the whole point of the sacrificial system.

God didn't require a sacrifice in order to forgive. The sacrifices were for the *Israelites*, not for God. He didn't forgive them *because* they made sacrifices. He asked them to make sacrifices *so they would know* they were forgiven.

Even now, God continues to assure us that he is friendly, not hostile and exacting. He knows that no one is harder on us than we are on ourselves—guilt and shame are powerful emotions! That's why he inspired John to write that "whenever our hearts condemn us," we should remember that "God is greater than our hearts, and he knows everything."[9] Because of the kind of person he is, we can "set our hearts at rest in his presence."[10] When we respond to his offer of friendship, we find that all our spiritual needs are taken care of.

God wants to give us more than we can imagine. I recently heard a speaker advise his audience not to spend too much time asking God to give us things. "After all," he said, "God isn't some heavenly Santa Claus." I thought about that for a moment and realized it's true. God isn't Santa Claus: God is *much more generous* than Santa Claus! Santa Claus is frightfully stingy compared to our generous God.

Don't ever be afraid to approach God and ask for things you want, even material things. He *wants* to give us more than we can imagine! This doesn't mean God will give us everything we ask for. He certainly won't give us things that he knows will harm us in some way. But there is no way we can out-ask his desire to give.

If you're thinking this couldn't possibly be true, check out the promise God gave to the Israelites as they journeyed on the way to the Promised Land: "The Lord your God will bring you into the land he promised to your ancestors, to Abraham, Isaac, and Jacob, and he will *give it to you.* The land has large, growing cities *you did not build,* houses full of good things *you did not buy,* wells *you did not dig,* and vineyards and olive trees *you did not plant.* You will eat as much as you want. But be careful! Do not forget the Lord, who brought you out of the land of Egypt where you were slaves."[11]

God longs to give us more than we can imagine, more than we could ever earn in a lifetime. He longs to pour out blessings and shower us with gifts. In this Bible passage, God promised a wealth of material things to the Israelites, *none of which they had worked for or earned.* God is not in the business of buying and selling; God is in the business of giving.

So, what's our part in this? Simply to receive and *remember.* Remembering is important. At the end of the promise, God says that when you're stuffed from eating and you're enjoying the high life, don't forget him. Don't let that old, ugly autonomy creep in and whisper that you acquired everything you have on your own. We should never forget that every good thing in our lives is a free gift from the hand of our generous God.

God takes care of all his children. In the Sermon on the Mount, Jesus said these curious words:

> You're familiar with the old written law, "Love your friend," and its unwritten companion, "Hate your enemy." I'm challenging that. I'm telling you to love your enemies. Let them bring out the best in you, not the worst. When someone gives you a hard time, respond with the energies of prayer, for then you are working out of your true selves, your God-created selves.
>
> This is what God does. He gives his best—the sun to warm and the rain to nourish—to *everyone*, regardless: the good and *bad*, the nice and *nasty*. If all you do is love the lov-

> able, do you expect a bonus? Anybody can do
> that. If you simply say hello to those who
> greet you, do you expect a medal? Any run-of-
> the-mill sinner does that.
>
> In a word, what I'm saying is, Grow up.
> You're kingdom subjects. Now live like it.
> Live out your God-created identity. Live *gener-*
> *ously and graciously toward others,* the way God
> lives toward you.[12]

God gives to *all* his children, the wicked ones and the righteous ones. He doesn't smile on the righteous and frown on the
wicked. He cares for everyone. *God treats all his children equally.* He
doesn't reward one group and punish another. He is a *giver.* Period.
He gives to *all,* the nice and the nasty.

For example, God is giving life to Satan right now, giving
him the opportunity to present his side of things in this war. God
sustains Satan's life; he doesn't have to, but he does because he's a
giver. He provides, even for the very worst of his children.

This should give us great confidence in God. We can know
that he will treat us with dignity and respect, regardless of how we
respond to him. *Even if we totally reject him,* God still gives us all he
can. Our God is not selfish. He is totally generous, and he has
shared *all* of himself with *all* of his children.

God is an all-out giver. He really can't help himself. And he invites us to join him in the circle of giving that leads to never-ending life: "The Father gave the Son; the Son gave the Spirit; the Spirit gives us life, so we can give the gift of love."[13]

And the gift goes on.

Show business

God's truth-in-advertising

Extraordinary claims require extraordinary evidence.
—*Carl Sagan*

Our world is a confusing jumble of true and false information. Information—much of it contradictory—comes at us from all directions: the media, the internet, the newspaper, our email inbox, and our friends, family, and co-workers. How easy is it to pick out the truth?

Here are four popular claims that have been making their way into email inboxes in recent years. Three of the claims are false; one is true. Can you spot the true claim?

1. Mobile homes are so named because they can be moved from place to place.

2. The nursery rhyme *Sing a Song of Sixpence* originated as a coded message used for recruiting pirates.

3. The Kentucky Fried Chicken chain changed its name to KFC in order to eliminate the word "fried" from its title.

4. The town of Tarzana, California, was named after the famous ape man.

Knowing which of these statements is true isn't really that important. To satisfy your curiosity, however, it's the one about the nursery rhyme. Of course, you could have gone your entire life without knowing that, and it wouldn't have mattered very much. But what about this next set of statements? One is true, and one is false. Do you know which is which?

1. God is a liar.

2. God tells the truth.

As you already know, this is the heart of the universal war on terror. We are accustomed to bloody wars on the battlefield, but the invisible war we're in is a war of ideas. How is such a war fought?

On one side, Satan just makes claims. He says all kinds of things about God, but he has no evidence to back up what he says. If God responded to Satan by also using claims, this war would be like a universal tiff between toddlers:

You're a liar!

No I'm not!

Yes you are!

No I'm not!

Are too!

Are not!

Too-too-too!

Not-not-not!

How can such an argument ever be settled once and for all? Evidence. That's right. In the universal game of show-and-tell, God does much more *showing* than he does telling. As a good attorney, he has successfully defended himself in the universal court of public opinion by providing evidence to refute Satan's claims. Satan has made many charges against God, and God has answered every one of them.

CHARGE #1: GOD IS VENGEFUL, HARSH, AND SEVERE

Exhibit A

God answered the accusation that he was vengeful[1] right off the bat by what he *didn't* do. Can you imagine Hitler or Stalin allowing any of their subordinates to openly bad-mouth them in public? If God had been the kind of person Satan claimed he was, Satan wouldn't have survived long enough to make his case.

At the very least, God would have publicly executed him in a forceful display of power. The very fact that Satan was allowed to make his case (and still does to this day) easily refutes the idea that God is vengeful, harsh, and severe.

Exhibit B

God continued his pattern of "non-action" evidence at the cross. When Jesus was taken away to be crucified, he was stripped, beaten, and strung up to die. What happened at Calvary is very important, but what about what *didn't* happen? There's God, hanging on the cross in supreme agony. He's tired, he's thirsty, and he's bleeding. He's struggling to breathe. People passing by spit on him and curse at him. They taunt him, calling for him to come down from the cross if he can.[2]

Here's the thing, though: *he could have come down from the cross.* Jesus had the power of the universe at his fingertips. He could have blinked his eyes and wiped out everyone in a hundred-mile radius. He could have twitched his eyebrow in just the right way, and a legion of angels would have come to his side. He could have done anything he wanted.

At the very least, he certainly could have *said* anything he wanted. He could have threatened his tormentors. He could have cursed at them. He could have told them that they were really gonna get it! But in his moment of utter blackness and total agony, what did God do? *He spoke forgiveness.*[3] He comforted his mother.[4] He encouraged the man who was dying next to him.[5] When God is abused, he doesn't get revenge. He forgives. He proved Satan was lying about him by what he *didn't* do at the cross.

CHARGE #2: GOD IS SELFISH

Exhibit A

Satan claimed God was a power-hungry tyrant who selfishly abused his power.[6] God answered this accusation by sharing his creative power with us. God designed us in his image to be a race of people who would have the ability to create little people in our own image.

God planned for this creation to take place in marriage between a man and a woman (a wonderful example that God's motivation for creating is love). Do you realize what that means? Our affections are to be partially directed toward another human being and not solely given to God. That doesn't sound like the actions of a selfish Creator!

Exhibit B

In Jesus, God demonstrated his selflessness repeatedly. For example, as the clock was ticking down toward his death, Jesus knelt down to wash the feet of his disciples. As they argued over who was going to be the greatest in God's kingdom, the Creator did the job of a slave. Hardly self-serving.

CHARGE #3: GOD IS LYING ABOUT DEATH

Exhibit A

In the whole course of human history, God has answered the accusation that he lied about death[7] with only one exhibit. This was a crucial case to build. Sin leads to death: God knew this, but that doesn't mean it would have been obvious to any of his other creatures. Nobody had ever seen *actual* death. Nobody really knew what it was.

So, once sin entered the universe, God needed to show where it would lead. He needed to prove that sin—*not him!*—causes death. *He wanted us to understand that he isn't going to execute sinners.*[8] There was only one way to accomplish such an exhibit: God would die first.

On the cross, Jesus died *actual* death, the sinner's death. Though he was on a cross when he died, Jesus didn't actually die from being crucified. He died from being totally separated from the Father. This is how he showed what sin does to us, because sin totally separates us from God. That's what Paul meant when he wrote, "Christ had no sin, but God made him become sin so that in Christ we could become right with God."[9]

While he was on the cross, Jesus made it clear that God was not torturing or "executing" him in any way. He said plainly that he was dying from being separated from the Source of Life. That's why he cried out, "My God, my God, why have you abandoned me?"[10] Jesus wanted us to know that God doesn't execute rebels. On the cross, Jesus proved that God told the truth: sin causes death.[11]

In this epic war, God provides evidence of the truth. He doesn't want us to believe anything based on claims—*even his own claims!* That means there is no such thing as "blind faith." Rather, our trust in God can be built on an intelligent understanding of the evidence he has provided time and time again. Beware of anyone who expects you to believe claims without evidence.*

One of the great things about God is that he is in the "show" business. He doesn't just expect us to go along with something because he "says so." In this world of confusing, contradictory information, our allegiance to God can be built on solid evidence. We don't have to wonder how he will treat us or try to guess how he will respond to us. Because of all the evidence he has provided in the past, we can trust him fully with the future.

---

* A shocking example of this is found in 1 Kings 13—definitely one of the scandals of the Bible!

God must be odd, 'cuz he never "gets even"

God's forgiveness

Love is an act of endless forgiveness, a tender look which becomes a habit.
—Peter Ustinov

At the end of a long, dusty day, the sun is setting. An old man squints through clouded eyes. He fears today will be no different from any other day, the days past stretching out into an endless stream of waiting and hoping.

Finally, he sighs and shakes his head. Just as he turns to go in for the night, something catches his eye. Frantic, he shades his eyes with a hand, squinting, straining, desperate to see if there is movement on the road.

There is.

With a shout, he leaps off the porch, running, flying as fast as he can on his crooked, old legs. One of his sandal straps breaks, but he doesn't even notice. He's running, crying, laughing, and screaming, racing toward the hunched-over, shuffling figure in the distance.

Jesus told this story of the boy who ran away with half his father's fortune, wasted it, and then came home.[1] It is usually called the Parable of the Prodigal Son. But the story is more about the *father* than the son.

In the culture and time when Jesus told this story, the son who ran away would never have been able to come home. His demand for his inheritance would have sounded like this: "Dad, I wish you were dead. Why don't you give me my inheritance now so I can leave, and we'll never have to see each other again." This would have been a grievous insult to his father, and his actions would have truly cut himself out of his family forever.

Yet when the son returns, Jesus said that the father saw him "while he was still a long way off."[2] That means the father must have been watching every day, waiting for his son to return. The father wouldn't have done that unless he had *forgiven the son long before he ever decided to come back.*

Could this be true? Could a father so grievously insulted wait with fervent longing for the return of his rebellious child? Yes! That is just how Jesus described the loving father. Though the son couldn't have imagined it, he was already forgiven. The father wasn't holding any grudge against his son. In fact, while the son was busy begging his father for forgiveness, the father wasn't listening. He was celebrating, shouting out party instructions to the servants.

One of the reasons Jesus told this story was to help us understand the way God forgives. He was describing himself as the father in the story!

When we embrace sin, we are overcome with guilt and shame, and we immediately become afraid of God. We're afraid he'll be angry with us. We're afraid he'll "make us pay" for what we've done. We're afraid he won't forgive.

Evidence to the contrary, however, is written all over the Bible. For example, after his resurrection, Jesus restored his friendship with Peter.* On the night of Jesus's trial, Peter denied three times that he even knew Jesus.[3] Immediately, Peter realized what he had done, and he was ashamed.

As soon as Jesus came out of the grave, he made a special point of singling Peter out[4] and reassuring him of his place in God's kingdom. Over breakfast one morning, Jesus pointedly asked Peter three times if he (Peter) loved him (Jesus). Doing this gave Peter a special opportunity to declare what he had denied.†

---

* Peter was one of Jesus's disciples and a leader in the early Christian church. He was hot-tempered and impulsive. He walked on water and cut off the ear of a soldier trying to arrest Jesus. Scholars believe he was martyred by Emperor Nero in AD 64.

† Read the whole, beautiful story in John, chapter 21.

On another occasion, the religious leaders brought to Jesus a woman who had been caught committing adultery.‡ They threw her down half-naked at his feet and asked him if they should stone her.[5]

Ignoring their question, Jesus stooped down and began to write in the sand. After a little while, he said that if any of them were sinless, they could throw the first stone at the woman. Then, he continued to write.

The Bible doesn't specify what Jesus was writing in the sand. Perhaps he was writing some secret sins these men had been hiding. Whatever it was, the religious leaders eventually slunk away. When they were gone, Jesus turned to the woman and said, "I don't condemn you, my daughter. Now go, and don't sin anymore."[6]

The point is that there are no barriers in God to his forgiving us. He freely forgives *because of who he is.* He doesn't forgive us just because we ask him to or even because we're willing to receive it. When Jesus was on the cross, his abusers didn't want his forgiveness. But he spoke forgiveness to them because *that's the kind of person he is.*

Forgiveness is letting go of the "right to get even" with a person who has hurt us in some way. And that's what God is like, because he never seeks to get even. His door is always open to us.[7]

---

‡ You can find this story in John, chapter 8.

No matter what we've done, God runs to meet us with open arms the moment he sees us coming. No matter how long we've been gone, the only thing that matters to God is that we're home again.

This quality of total forgiveness in God means that *he has even forgiven Satan* for everything Satan has done. This idea might be confusing and even unpleasant for some. We might wonder if this is true. Jesus said clearly that Satan and his angels could not be saved.[8] Can God forgive those who can't be saved? Of course. *Salvation is achieved through friendship, not forgiveness.*

For centuries, Christians have mistakenly believed that salvation was about finding a way to get God to forgive our sins. That's not true. Forgiveness isn't the obstacle to salvation. The obstacle to salvation is our unwillingness to trust God. If we embrace an attitude of distrust and fear toward God, we will refuse to have a relationship with him.

God freely forgives, but this forgiveness can't affect us if we aren't willing to receive it. The sad thing is that Satan and all of God's other wicked children will die having been totally forgiven, but they won't know it. In the same way, if the prodigal son had sat in the pigpen until he starved, he would have died having been totally forgiven by his father. He wouldn't have known it, though, because he never would have gone home to find out.

God wants to reshape our thinking on forgiveness. He wants us to learn how to see "vengeance" like he does. Paul lays it out in Romans 12:

> Don't insist on getting even; that's not for you to do. "I'll do the judging," says God. "I'll take care of it."
>
> Our Scriptures tell us that if you see your enemy hungry, go buy that person lunch, or if he's thirsty, get him a drink. Your generosity will surprise him with goodness. Don't let evil get the best of you; get the best of evil by doing good.[9]

Some suggest that God asks us to do the latter part—feeding and clothing our enemies—so he can take care of the judgment and wrath. They say this as if God is really looking forward to making his evil children suffer, and he wants to relish that task all by himself.

That's ridiculous! God doesn't hold us to a different standard than himself. He never lets evil get the best of him, and he's eager to educate us in his method of "getting even." *Overcoming evil with good:* that's almost the very definition of God. He always repays evil with *blessings*.

If you're drowning in guilt and fear over the bad choices you've made in your life, don't be afraid. You *can* get up and go home. You are *already* forgiven! God is an *immediate* forgiver. He'll welcome you with open arms and treat you like you never left. In him, there are no obstacles to forgiveness.

Look who's stalking

God's initiation

A true initiation never ends.
—Robert Anton Wilson

In the Garden of Eden.

To Cain, the murderer.

To Noah, the shipbuilder.

In the land of Egypt.

In the Sinai wilderness.

To Nebuchadnezzar, the king.

In a prophet's dream.

In a teenager's womb.

The Bible is the story of God and how he keeps coming.

Adam and Eve's choice to rebel ignited an immediate fear of God in their hearts. They ate the fruit, and before they even knew why, they hid. They were afraid of what God was going to do.

And what did God do? He came. He came looking for them. Certainly, he knew where they were. He could have surprised them, scared them, and overwhelmed them. Instead, he let his soft footfalls fill the garden air as he called out, "Where are you?"[1] He came, and he did everything he could to ease their fears.

Centuries later, God told a prophet named Hosea* to marry an unfaithful wife.† So he married Gomer, and they started having children together. She also had children by other men. Often, she ran away from Hosea, and Hosea would go after her, wooing her until she came back home again. God used this real-life soap opera to teach the Israelites about his love for them.

At one point in the story, God told Hosea, "Start all over: Love your wife again, your wife who's in bed with her latest boyfriend, your cheating wife. Love her the way I, God, love the Israelite people, even as they flirt and party with every god that takes their fancy."[2]

Hosea pursued Gomer repeatedly until, at last, she settled down with him and never ran away again. Hosea's initiation paid off; God hopes his initiation will pay off, too.

---

* The prophet Hosea lived in the eighth century BC during the reign of Jeroboam II. Though this was a time of material prosperity for Israel, there was a lot of fear and anxiety among the nations. Hosea called for spiritual reform in the land of Israel, trying to get people to return to God.

† You can read all about Hosea and Gomer in Hosea, chapters 1-4.

Centuries after Hosea wooed Gomer, God showed up in Bethlehem—not as a husband, not as a Creator playing hide and seek, but as a baby. God came to our planet as a human being, and he was still doing everything he could to ease our fears.

John later wrote about it this way: "The Word became flesh and made his dwelling among us. *We have seen his glory*, the glory of the One and Only, who came from the Father, *full of grace and truth*."[3]

Through his life and death on this planet, Jesus proved that we have nothing to fear from God. We were the ones who rebelled. We alienated ourselves from God. We strained our relationship with him.

But God didn't wait for us to apologize. He turned our "offense" against him into an occasion to go "on the offensive" with us. Even in his death on the cross, he was saying, "I want you to know the truth about me. *I would rather die* than live without you forever."

Our relationship with God is at the top of his priority list. He leaves no stone unturned and spares no expense in his efforts to woo us back to him. It's fortunate for us that God is such an outrageous lover. If he wasn't, how could we ever hope to find him? How could we begin to repair our relationship with him, even if we wanted to?

In our lost and wayward condition—blind, deaf, mute, and stuck in the quicksand of sin—the fact that *God* continues to come to *us* is our lifeline. And he will continue this initiation as long as there is the slightest chance that we might turn around and go home with him.

Whether his advances are accepted or rejected, God keeps coming. He shakes off rejection like Superman flicking off a flea, and he keeps coming. As long as there is any hope for our salvation, he keeps coming. This sounds quite intense, and it is! As long as there is any chance we'll accept him, God continues to pursue us.

Ultimately, though, God won't chain us up and throw us in his basement. If we prefer not to have a relationship with him, God will respect that choice. However, until we make that decision and say "final answer," he will go to the ends of the earth to pursue us.

As David said, "Where can I go to get away from your Spirit? Where can I run from you? If I go up to the heavens, you are there. If I lie down in the grave, you are there. If I rise with the sun in the east and settle in the west beyond the sea, even there you would guide me. With your right hand, you would hold me."[4]

What a beautiful picture of God. No matter where we go, he's waiting around every corner. He's under every rock. He's right behind every door, eager to scoop us up and show us how good it is to be with him.

He doesn't act this way because we've asked for it or earned it. He pursues us like this because he's a lover. It's who he is.

No matter how many times we've rejected him, God pursues us. No matter how much pain we've caused him, God loves us. No matter how loudly we've disowned him, God chooses us. He's hoping we'll choose him, too.

Heaven can wait

God's patience

Patience is not passive, but active; it is concentrated strength.
—Edward G. Bulwer-Lytton

Good things come to those who wait. God certainly knows the value of this famous phrase. For many centuries, he has played the waiting game as we creep along in our understanding of him, one millimeter at a time. It's a long road.

Though he exists beyond the reaches of Time, God has willingly subjected himself to the linear timeline of our world. From creation to this day, God engages with us *where we are*—in our time and space, though he is infinitely beyond both.

Consider the major time prophecies of the Bible. With his universal 20/20 vision, God detailed future events for his people with incredible accuracy.

To the prophets Daniel* and Isaiah and to the apostle John, God described events that wouldn't take place until long after they were dead and buried. Thousands of years later, we can look back and see that God knew exactly what he was talking about. Each event came to fulfillment at precisely the time he said it would. All the while, God has waited *thousands* of years for our planet's history to unfold. Why?

The Process of Relationship

God's work with us is relational, which is always a process. While God is interested in the conclusions we form about him, he is even more interested in the *process* by which we form them. God is not interested in our knowing the truth if he has to convey it in a way that destroys our relationship or overrides our freedom.

Our understanding of truth is progressive. Since God *is* truth, that means our understanding of him is *also* progressive. He reveals the truth about himself to us through our relationship.

We learn more about him as our relationship deepens. Because we are so slow to understand, this requires a lot of patience on God's part.

---

* The prophet Daniel lived during the time Israel was in exile in Babylon. While he was a slave in King Nebuchadnezzar's court, Daniel became famous for the ability to interpret dreams. The Old Testament Bible book Daniel chronicles his story and is full of prophecy.

Respecting Our Response

Because God values friendship and freedom, he takes our responses seriously. This includes acceptance and rejection. If God only wanted slaves, he could totally disregard our responses. It wouldn't matter whether we accepted or rejected him.

If God wanted slaves, it would only matter that we do what he said when he said it. In fact, rejecting him wouldn't even be an option. If God didn't care about freedom, he could do whatever he wanted without regard for anyone but himself, for who could oppose him?

But God *does* care. He wants friends, not servants. And no two friendships are the same. That's why he treats each one of us as unique. Instead of expecting us to conform ourselves to him, *he customizes his approach to us* based on our responses. He knows us inside and out. He knows our very thoughts, and he works with each of us in a unique way. This is why Jesus warned us not to judge others.[1]

I can't expect God to deal with another person in exactly the same way as me any more than I would expect a parent of five children to relate to each one in precisely the same way. Parenting methods are adjusted according to the needs of the child. In the same way, God makes allowances for our individual differences. He deals with us according to what he knows is best for us.

An Emerging Maturity

When we are in a relationship with God, we can expect to understand him better every step of the way. Paul said, "God began doing a good work in you, and I am sure he will continue it until it is finished when Jesus Christ comes again."[2]

Elsewhere, he called Jesus "the champion who initiates and perfects our faith."[3] God begins his work in us by initiating a relationship with us. Then, he graciously leads us—no faster than we are able or willing to go—ever deeper into that relationship, finishing what he started.

As we continue in our relationship with God, we can also expect to undergo a process of emerging maturity in our faith. Jesus himself said, "I have many more things to say to you, but they are too much for you now."[4]

Imagine how much God has to say to us! Imagine how much he wants to teach us about life and love and the way things are really meant to be! And while you're imagining that, remember that he knows you intimately and is willing to take as much time as you need to help you understand what you need to know.

It's similar to learning calculus. You wouldn't try to teach calculus to a three-year-old. A toddler has to learn concepts in sequence: first letters and numbers, then addition, subtraction, multiplication, division, fractions, and so forth. Somewhere along the line, the child must also transition from dealing exclusively with concrete objects to processing abstract thought.

We don't expect kindergarteners to perform calculus. However, we have designed an educational system that brings them gradually to the place where they can. This is just how God works with us.

It's amazing, isn't it? The God who is beyond Time comes and walks alongside us, submitting himself to *our* learning curve. We don't have to worry about being left in the dust; God is infinitely patient. He'll never take us any faster than we are able or willing to go.

On guard

God's protectiveness

Our safe place is not where we live; it is in whom we live.
—*Tom White*

By nature, God is a mama bear. As a perfect parent, God is fiercely protective of his children. He has spared nothing (even his own life) in the fight against sin and death, the intruders in his creation. He has left no stone unturned in his plan to save his children and restore peace to the universe.

God is a perfect parent, but parenting isn't easy. Frequently, it involves making tough decisions—the kind of decisions that cause pain for the parent. Parenting is fraught with challenges and is not for the feint of heart. At times, parents have to be willing to make the tough choices.

It's the same for God. You think three children are hard to handle? Try *billions*. Then, throw a raging war in the mix with a loudmouthed opponent who goes around trying to convince your children to be afraid of you, and you can begin to grasp God's predicament. For a lesser parent, this might be a problem.

God, however, has always been willing to make the tough choices, especially when the tough choices protect us from the ultimate enemy (death). Of course, like most children, we whine about these choices, ignore them, or even rebel against them. The fact remains, however, that everything God has done since the beginning of human history has been for our protection.

The Law

God protected us from rushing headlong into irreversible rebellion by giving us "the law." Have you ever read the book of Deuteronomy? It's full of all the laws God gave to the Israelites after he rescued them from Egypt. They're interesting.

Some still make sense to us today: *Don't murder.*[1]

Some make no sense to us today: *If a murder occurs that goes unsolved, the leaders from the nearest town must take a cow to the place where the body was found and break its neck.*[2]

And there are some we would probably like to reinstate: *At the end of every seven years, all debts must be canceled.*[3]

God gave these laws to the Israelites because they needed them. Spiritually, these adults were *infants*.* At one point, they expressed the desire to return to brutal slavery in Egypt because they weren't satisfied with what God was feeding them in the wilderness.[4] They had no concept of right and wrong. After living for four hundred years in a land with people who worshipped hundreds of gods, they weren't inclined to listen to or believe in one, true God.

What would you do if your toddler was determined to run out into a busy city street? Would you be willing to take some drastic measures? Perhaps you might do things that wouldn't conform to the image of a loving parent. I'm willing to bet that you would do *whatever it took* to keep your child out of the street, because disciplining your child—even in a harsh manner—is certainly better than your child getting run over by a car.

That's what God had to do with the Israelites, only the landscape was more abstract. He was trying to save them from *spiritual* death, not physical death. In a spiritual sense, they were determined to run out blindly into the street. So, to keep them from rushing headlong into total rebellion, he set up some very harsh, very strict boundaries.

---

* The next time you read through the Old Testament stories of the Israelites in the wilderness, consider this: though "adults" by age, this was a group of millions of emotionally- and spiritually-immature children—temper tantrum-throwing two-year-olds. And God was just trying to get them to pay attention long enough so he could take them into the Promised Land.

Those boundaries served a healthy purpose until Jesus came. His life was the fulfillment of the law. That means that by his example, we can clearly see right from wrong, including the truth about God. Jesus said, "Don't misunderstand why I have come. I did not come to abolish the law of Moses or the writings of the prophets. No, I came to accomplish their purpose."[5]

When asked which law was most important, Jesus said it was most important to love God with all your heart and to love your neighbor as yourself.[6] In fact, he said that every law previously given to humanity was an extension of those two principles.

If we followed those principles, we would be practicing other-centeredness. That's love. *Love* is the center of the law. Jesus didn't do away with the law. *He is* the center of the law! God didn't give us the law so we'd have a list of rules to keep. He gave us the law so we could practice love.

Because of Jesus's testimony, we know that it's not about following the "letter of the law." God is after *love*, and love can't be legislated. We could follow the letter of the law all our lives and *never* arrive at love. But there is no way that we can love and *not* end up following the spirit of the law.

Every law God ever gave was to keep us from devoting ourselves to rebellion before he could lead us to love. Paul said that before Jesus came, "we were held in custody under the law, locked up until the faith that was to come would be revealed."[7] Held *in custody* by the law? Locked up? Exactly! God used the law as a *restraint*, a boundary, until Jesus could come to give us the full, flesh-and-blood picture of love.

And this love leads us right into life. It's ironic, isn't it? That the law—which we normally associate with restriction—actually frees us up to pursue life! God gave the law to free us, not enslave us. My daughter Claire stated this so well in a card she sent to me following her teenage years when her mother and I had set some strong boundaries at home. She wrote, "Thank you for protecting me, dad. Your guidance and safeguarding in my life have enabled me to be bold and courageous in the path I am now pursuing."

This is the experience God intended us to have with the law. His apparent "restrictions" are always designed to enable us to move out into a bold, courageous, and free life.

The First Death

God protected us from the foolish idea of autonomy by subjecting us to the first death.† Every human being is subject to the death that occurs on this planet.

---

† The "first death," which is sleep, as opposed to the "second death," which is extinction.

In God's universe, which is based on natural laws and consequences, the first death is an imposter. It's an in-between state. It's not really death (in its final and very ugly form), but it's certainly not conscious life either. God uses it, however, to teach us that *no created being can be autonomous.* Nobody can decide *not* to die. Furthermore, most of us have no control over when and how that death comes to us.

You've heard the saying that there are only two certainties in this life: death and taxes. Depending on how clever your accountant is, you may find ways to avoid taxes. But you have absolutely no wiggle room on the first death. You will eventually face the fact that you're dependent, that you can't sustain your own life.

This is one of the reasons God instituted the first death. For some of us, the realization that we are not autonomous may be the only thing that turns us in God's direction. It may be the only thing that saves us from true, irreversible death. If so, it's worth it.

The Sabbath

God protected us from trivializing his place in our life by giving us the Sabbath.‡ In a war, it's hard to keep your wits about

---

‡ The Sabbath is a day of rest specifically designed by God at the end of creation. During the first Sabbath, God rested from all the work of creating he had done, and he invited us to join him in his rest.

you. Bombs fall at random. The distant crack of gunshots shatters the silence. Fear is a constant companion. People who live in a war zone long for peace, security, and a few moments of quiet. They long to remember when times were better.

Though it's hidden from our sight, we should try to remember that we live in a war zone. We shouldn't forget that we have an adversary described as a roaring lion who prowls around looking for someone to devour.[8] Most of the time, though, we're too busy to think about that war. We're always on the go. We run around at breakneck speed in the "rat race," trying to accomplish everything on our never-ending lists. It seems the more timesaving devices we get, the less time we have. It's never enough. Maybe we also long for peace, security, and a few moments of quiet. Maybe we long to remember the good times.

God has designed just such a time for us. At the very end of creation week, God made a gift for his newly created friends, Adam and Eve. He carved out a gift of time. God created the Sabbath to be a multi-dimensional gift. He created it so we could rest and relax. He created it to give us some built-in relational time with him. But God also designed the Sabbath to protect us from trivializing his place in our life.

The Sabbath is an interesting "law" because the reasons given for observing it appear to shift over time. The first time the Sabbath is mentioned, the Bible simply states that God blessed it and set it apart by resting from all the work of creating that he had just done.[9]

The Sabbath isn't mentioned again until God gave the Ten Commandments to the people of Israel. In that account, the people were asked to keep the Sabbath day holy, remembering that God was the one who created the heavens and the earth.[10]

Later, the Israelites were reminded again to keep the Sabbath day holy. This time, however, they were invited to remember that God had rescued them from Egypt, thereby saving them from a life of slavery.[11] And Jesus added to it by saying that humans shouldn't observe Sabbath for God's sake alone, but for their own sake.[12]

It is clear, then, that God intended the Sabbath to be a day of remembering. At first, that may sound odd, but because our lives are so hectic, we easily *forget* our place in the world. With careers and family, it's easy to fall into the mindset that we are independent. We start thinking we've got it all together—we can provide for ourselves. It is so easy to forget about God and his role in our lives. It is so easy to forget that everything we have—every breath we take—is a gift from him. Were it not for the Sabbath, we may start believing we've got it all under control.

On the Sabbath, however, God invites us to remember. We may remember that he is the Creator, that he designed everything we enjoy. We may remember, as the Israelites did, that God worked miracles in Egypt and that he rescues us from much more than we ever give him credit for. We may remember that Jesus rested in the tomb on the Sabbath after he died on the cross, and we may reflect on the meaning of all he said and did during his life here on Earth. We may remember specific instances from our own lives where we have seen God's working or felt God's presence in our circumstances. He works in all things today just as surely as he did six thousand years ago.

If we decide we're too busy to observe God's Sabbath day, we're the ones who lose the blessing. Of course, God also misses the pleasure of our company. Any parent who has lived through a holiday season without having the entire family home again knows the disappointment God must feel when we're not together with him on his special day. But God doesn't hold that against us. He looks for other ways to bless us, other ways to bring peace and rest into our lives.

Still, the accumulated weight of God's acts of love through history can only be felt in a special way during a Sabbath time of remembrance. God is eager for us to receive his greatest blessings. That's why he wants us to accept his invitation to join him in resting on the Sabbath. In the war zone we live in, the Sabbath is God's best weapon against fear, insecurity, and forgetting the one who loves us so much.

Suffering

God protects us for eternity by not protecting us from suffering in the here and now. It's a strange idea, isn't it? God protects us by *not* protecting us. Exploring the opposite notion may provide a better picture. God could protect the whole universe from suffering. But the only way for him to do that would be to *remove all the consequences of sin*. God hates suffering. He hurts when we hurt, but removing the consequences of sin forever would turn us into robots.

Removing the consequences of our rebellion would be a denial of our freedom. We wouldn't really be free to choose if God wouldn't allow us to experience the results of our choice. So, the existence of suffering in the universe proves that we really are free to choose and that God takes our freedom seriously. Furthermore, if he removed the consequences of sin, we would never understand that sin is deadly. How could God win the war if he removed the evidence about the nature of sin?

Of course, we see things differently than God. Elisabeth Elliot, in her book *Passion and Purity*, expresses our position perfectly:

> Our vision is so limited that we can hardly
> imagine a love that does not show itself in
> protection from suffering. The love of God is
> of a different nature altogether. It does not

hate tragedy. It never denies reality. It stands
in the very teeth of suffering. The love of God
did not protect his own Son.

That was the proof of his love—that he
gave that Son, that he let him go to Calvary's
cross, though "legions of angels" might have
rescued him. He will not necessarily protect
us—not from anything it takes to make us like
his Son. A lot of hammering and chiseling and
purifying by fire will have to go into the process.[13]

Though we don't like to suffer, we can understand that rebellious choices lead to suffering. On some level, it's normal for us
to believe that we *deserve* to suffer. We know that if we "do the
crime," we have to "do the time." That's why it's absolutely remark-
able to discover that God suffers right along with us!

Though God wasn't responsible for sin, he hasn't insulated
himself from the suffering *we* have caused. In fact, by allowing freedom in his universe, God has placed himself squarely in the fire. As
a perfect parent, God suffers when his children suffer. That means
he has suffered more than anyone since the beginning of the war.

God doesn't suffer without cause, however. Allowing the
consequences of sin to be openly demonstrated is how God protects us from ultimate self-destruction. When we feel the suffering

that comes as a result of sin, and when we see the effects of sin in the world, we are able to see clearly that God tells the truth about the nature of sin. We see it for the awful thing it is, and it makes us run straight for God.

Think back again to the story of the prodigal son. He had a great time wasting all his money. But if he had never faced the consequences of his foolishness, he might never have gone home. In his case, the discomfort of the pigpen was ultimately a *blessing*.

This planet has turned into our pigpen. Being forced to wallow around in the pig slop, while painful, is worth it if it motivates us to get up and go home. The alternative is that we would never go home. And being separated from God forever is *far* worse than some temporary discomfort.

While God doesn't remove suffering in this life, he does promise to be with us every step of the way: "When you pass through the waters, I will be with you. When you pass through the rivers, they will not flow over you. When you walk through the fire, you will not be burned. The fire will not destroy you."[14]

You see, God doesn't promise us a way out. Instead, he promises us a way *through*, with him right beside. Hasn't he kept that promise? He didn't leave us to deal with sin on our own. Instead, God came and personally took on our suffering and death in order to show us the way to life.

In that same Bible passage, God promises our suffering won't be permanent. We will pass through rivers, but we won't ultimately drown. We'll walk in the fire, but we won't ultimately be destroyed. Allowing us to experience suffering with him now is one of the ways he protects us against rushing headlong into total destruction.

Every gift from God is good, even the ones we don't like. He spares nothing—even his own comfort—to protect us from the ultimate consequences of sin.

Because of this, we can have great confidence that God is working through all of life's circumstances to bring about our best good. This should help us to say, along with Paul, that we can and will "give thanks in all circumstances."[15]

Frequently asked questions

God's self-assurance

The beauty of enmity is insecurity; the beauty of friendship is in security.
—*Robert Frost*

Do you think too much about whether others like you or not? Do you try to conform yourself to what you think others want you to be? Are you addicted to approval?

If so, have you ever wished you didn't feel so insecure? Have you ever wanted to just be confident and at peace with yourself, with nothing to prove to the world? If so, that was a piece of the image of God within you, struggling to get out. That's what God is like.

God exists in a state of total security (the opposite of *insecurity*) because he lives with the truth. He has nothing to fear and nothing to hide from. He is true to himself, he is consistent, and he always works in the best interests of others. Though God would like to be accepted by all his creatures, he is not crushed by rejection. He's a powerhouse of self-assurance.

Since we are completely insecure, we buck against authority and push the boundaries. We do this to find out where we stand in relationship to authority, just as little children do. God graciously accepts our questions, even welcomes them. He is pleased when we will engage with him, even if we approach him from a position of insecurity. Since he harbors no self-doubt, God is able to creatively respond to our needs.

God encourages us to understand him. He works in ways that appeal to our reason. His friends throughout the Bible asked him questions, even appeared to argue with him at times. *God likes that.* In fact, Jesus said he prefers relationships that include the exchange of important information.[1]

Job* was God's friend, and he was accustomed to having open conversations with God. Because of this friendship, Satan began a campaign of suffering in Job's life. He killed Job's family, stripped him of his wealth, and attacked his health. Even after losing it all, however, Job seemed most bothered by God's silence. Job cried out, "Call, and I will answer. Or let me speak, and you answer

---

* Job's story is described in the Old Testament Bible book of Job, which is commonly believed to be one of the earliest-written Bible books. Nobody knows for sure when Job lived, but scholars speculate it was sometime between 2100 BC and 1700 BC.

me."[2] Of all the things Job lost, his dialogue with God was the most important to him.

God is pleased when we are eager to engage with him. Once, Daniel was confused about a vision he had received. He didn't understand what it meant, so he asked God to explain it to him. Almost immediately, an angel appeared and said, "Daniel, I have come here to give you insight and understanding. The moment you began praying, a command was given. And now I am here to tell you what it was, for you are very precious to God. Listen carefully so that you can understand the meaning of your vision."[3]

Daniel was no more precious to God than we are. God is eager to give us understanding and insight about the things in our life that perplex and confuse us.

God wants us to understand him. He wants us to ask questions about why he runs things like he does. God invites us to come and reason with him,[4] and he willingly accepts us in any condition.

In his letter to the Romans, Paul observed that the people who weren't even trying to gain God's favor found that he had accepted them.[5] God eagerly welcomes us, whether we are angry, hurt, joyful, or frustrated. Because he's totally secure in himself, God has infinite patience to work with us.

We see this most clearly in the life of Jesus as he dealt with the religious leaders in his day. They hated Jesus, and they were always looking for ways to trap him. One day, they asked him a question about taxes:

> They came to him and said, "Teacher, we know that you are an honest man. You are not afraid of what other people think about you, because you pay no attention to who they are. And you teach the truth about God's way. Tell us: Is it right to pay taxes to Caesar or not? Should we pay them, or not?"
>
> But knowing what these men were really trying to do, Jesus said to them, "Why are you trying to trap me? Bring me a coin to look at." They gave Jesus a coin, and he asked, "Whose image and name are on the coin?"
>
> They answered, "Caesar's."
>
> Then Jesus said to them, "Give to Caesar the things that are Caesar's, and give to God the things that are God's." The men were amazed at what Jesus said.[6]

Jesus knew what these guys were up to. He knew they were trying to find a way to get rid of him. But because he was totally secure in the knowledge of who he was, Jesus wasn't bothered by this at all. He creatively interacted with these insecure religious leaders instead of trying to defend himself. And they were amazed.

It is true that, in our insecurity, we try to push the boundaries in order to find out where we stand in relationship to authority. With God, the astounding truth we discover is that this Authority, who could make us slaves, lifts us up instead and puts us in friendship with him. His security totally dissolves our insecurity.

Unconditional surrender

God's wrath

Who would believe divine wrath involves surrender?
—Anonymous

Here's the essence of God's wrath: in a universe where both freedom and sin are realities, surrender is a foregone conclusion. Either we surrender to God and allow him to heal us from sin, or he will eventually surrender us to sin and the death it causes.

Either we surrender, or he surrenders. Astonishingly, we are the ones who make the call. As C.S. Lewis put it so succinctly in his book *The Great Divorce*, "There are only two kinds of people in the end: those who say to God, 'Thy will be done,' and those to whom God says, in the end, '*Thy* will be done.'"[1]

Both groups will stand before God on that day. And right now, little by little, day by day, we are choosing which group we will belong to. The Bible refers to these two groups of people as the righteous and the wicked, but they could just as easily be called the free and the slaves.

You see, the wicked group will have completely surrendered themselves to rebellion. They will be utterly incapable of turning around and embracing life. By their persistent rebellion, they will have obliterated their freedom to choose anything other than death.

What a tragedy! The statement of ultimate love is "I would rather die than live without you forever." But the statement of ultimate rebellion is "I would rather die than live a life forever dependent on you, God." That's the essence of sin. In the process of striving for total independence, sin leaves God's intelligent creatures incapable of making free choices—it totally enslaves its followers to selfishness and death.

That's why sin is so awful. It turns true freedom into real slavery. The irony of sin is that it strives for autonomy, but instead creates automatons. Sin appears to promote freedom, but instead, it ends in a pit of total enslavement. No wonder God hates it so much and will do anything to keep us from it.

It isn't easy to become part of this wicked group. God makes it very, very hard. This isn't something we hear often, but it's true: *It is not easy to be lost!* We may have an inclination toward rebellion, but God makes it *very* difficult for us to continue in that path.

He throws obstacles in our way. He constructs huge *Detour* signs. He builds walls to keep us from going farther. We have to *really work at* being lost. We have to constantly turn God away—again and again and again.

So, in the end, those who are in the group with the wicked will only be there because *that's where they want to be.* Though God will respect our freedom to reject him if we want to, he makes it *very* hard to be lost.

Once the wicked have reached the point of no return in their rebellion and are totally enslaved to sin, God will honor their choice and let them go. When he does, they will fall into the chasm of sin's self-destruction. That will be awful, and it will be permanent.

Sin causes extinction—*true* death. It's the death from which there is no return. That's why God fights until the very end. He refuses to surrender as long as there is any possibility that his rebellious children could turn around and embrace life.

In this universal war on terror, Satan has succeeded in leaving us with the impression that God is the one who destroys the wicked. Satan has claimed that if we don't love God and serve him, he will destroy us.

Satan wants us to believe that there will come a time when God draws a line in the sand and says, "Enough. Now I will destroy you because you rejected me." Satan has profited immensely from this lie—it has turned many people away from God.

If we believe this about God, if we believe that he is the kind of person who would say, "Love me, or I'll kill you," then we begin to fear him. It's a subtle fear. We may not even perceive it at first, but it's there. We know we'd better stay in line—or else.

The problem with this is that fear is the enemy of trust. If we're afraid of God, we're not going to trust him. We're not going to listen to what he says, and we certainly won't *do* what he says. Well, we might obey at first because we're afraid, but over time, that fear will turn to rebellion. That's exactly what Satan wants. His lies about God are designed to lead us to fear and rebellion.

We have nothing to fear from God. God is good, not evil. God is life, not death. God is mercy, not vengeance. God is justice, not retribution. God is love, and when true love has been spurned, it doesn't *destroy* the object of its affection. Rather, true love works hard to win back what it has lost.

In the end, however, if love is unsuccessful, *love lets go*. This is God's wrath as described by Paul in Romans. He says that, in the end, God runs out of patients, not patience.[2] This is precisely what Jesus demonstrated on the cross.[3]

When God does let go, the Bible calls it his "strange work."[4] This is because the idea of "giving up" is foreign to love. Love doesn't give up! Love bears all things, believes all things, keeps going to the end, and never looks back.* That's why God refuses to surrender until there is absolutely nothing more he can do.

It's astounding that God's commitment to freedom is so great that he will engage in a "strange work" that will rip his heart out. Though it's agony for him to let go, he treats even his wicked children with dignity and respect. He won't ignore their freedom in order to shield himself from suffering.

Surrendering his wicked children to self-destruction is absolute torture for God, who created them and loves them. In Hosea 11:8, God screams, "How, oh how, can I give you up? How, oh how, can I let you go? My heart recoils at the very thought of it!"[5]

Even in the midst of this agony, however, God respects the choices of his wicked children and lets them go. Paul describes it as God giving them up and handing them over to their sinful desires.[6]

But God doesn't reserve this surrender only for the wicked. In Revelation, John says that God's righteous children are *also* given up to their choice—life. At the end, God says that *everybody* will be left alone to keep doing what they have chosen to do—the righteous will keep on being righteous, and the wicked will keep on being wicked.[7]

---

* Read more about love in 1 Corinthians, chapter 13.

God knows when all his children have made their choices. That's what he's patiently waiting for. God doesn't want any of his children to die, so he's willing to wait as long as it takes. He will know when the righteous are settled into the truth and the wicked are settled into the lie.

And when everyone has made their final decisions, given their "final answer," the war will end. Both sides will have made their presentations, the evidence will have been displayed, and all of God's children will have made their verdicts.

With no point in prolonging the war any further, God will surrender us to the consequences of our choices. Those who have chosen God will be handed over to the freedom of life. Those who have chosen sin will be handed over to the slavery of death.

This is God's wrath—recognizing our choices and surrendering us to them. His wrath is nothing like human anger. It is surrender.

Unfortunately, God will undoubtedly face the painful realization that—though he has won the war—he has lost many children. On that day, he will face the worst possible kind of pain—that of a parent losing a child—as he surrenders *himself* and us to the choices we have made.

Keeping our options open

God's commitment to freedom

The love of liberty is the love of others.
——*William Hazlitt*

Of all God's character traits, his commitment to freedom is the most important. Freedom is the foundation of everything God does, and he insists on keeping it at any price.

In fact, freedom was so important to God, he subjected himself to suffering and death in order to preserve it. Why is freedom so important? Consider this diagram:

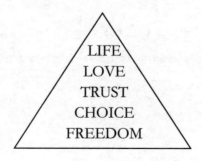

Intelligent life cannot exist without freedom. Freedom is the foundation of the created universe, the principle on which all other attributes rest. That's why it's at the bottom of the diagram. Everything else is built on it. If you remove freedom from the pyramid, intelligent life would cease.

Freedom supports choice. Without freedom, there would be no choice. We would be robots or slaves, unable to choose to either love God or reject him. Although we wouldn't know we were robots, there would be no opportunity for mutual love or friendship. Instead of living forever with understanding friends, God would have races of robotic animals designed to fulfill his needs.

Choice supports trust. Without choice, there would be no trust. If we weren't really free to choose rebellion, how could we trust God? If God annihilated his enemies, we would spend an eternity cowering in fear. That fear may keep us in line, but it wouldn't produce trust.

Trust supports love. Without trust, there would be no love, because genuine love can only develop in an atmosphere of trust. If a man proposed to his girlfriend and followed up his "Will you marry me?" with "You realize, though, that if you ever leave me, I'll find you and kill you," we would advise that girl to file for a restraining order instead of a marriage license. Nobody in their right mind would encourage a girl to marry a man who would threaten to kill her!

Love supports life. Without love, there would be no life. Life is an interdependent process that requires unselfish give-and-take. Selfish taking leads to death, not life. Selfishness self-destructs. We are dependent on others, and others are dependent on us. If we don't give *and* take, life ceases.

Freedom is the underpinning of the whole operation. That's why God is totally committed to freedom. He's committed to providing the ongoing opportunity to choose. And he is committed to respecting our choices, even when that means he loses his children to rebellion and self-destruction.

The fact that we are in this universal war is evidence that our freedom is a reality. If God didn't care about freedom, he wouldn't have put himself through the pain and suffering this war has caused him. He wouldn't have said that he preferred friends over slaves. He wouldn't have created us with the option of rebelling in the first place. Instead, he would have created a nice, obedient bunch of robots designed to pamper him.

The amazing and wonderful thing about God is that he *wants* love. He wants freedom. He wants intelligent creatures who understand him and *choose* to be his friends based on that understanding. That's why he didn't throw his hands up in the air and say "Forget it!" when we rebelled. He came right into the middle of our mess and fought to win us back.

He will fight until the very end, but he won't force us to choose him. Ultimately, the God who is all-powerful grants *us* the power to make the most important choice in life: will we live or will we die? God certainly has a vested interest—he wants us all to live![1] But what he wants even more than our living is our *choosing*.[2] While God prefers that we choose life, the *choice* is the most important aspect to him. He wants us free to choose.

What's more, on top of giving us the power to choose, God doesn't punish us if we make a choice he doesn't like. He treats us with kindness and respect, even if we reject him. He treats his righteous children no differently than his wicked children. Yes, it's true. God doesn't destroy his enemies! Understanding this about him is what secures our freedom forever.

Nobody knows better than God that freedom isn't free. Like a mighty warrior, he strode right into the middle of the conflict. He sacrificed *himself* to win the war. God is the original Freedom Fighter. Because of who he is and all he's done, love has unraveled fear, and freedom wins the day.

Happily ever after

The end of the war

True love doesn't have a happy ending—true love doesn't end.
—Unknown

Someday soon, the war will end. And it will end as it began: with the freedom to choose. God has fought down through the ages, sparing nothing—even his own life—to secure this freedom for the entire universe.

When the war finally ends, God will honor the choices we have made. Those who want to be in his presence will have their wish granted. They will live forever. Those who can't stand to be in his presence will have their wish granted. They will be no more.

From one end of the universe to the other, all creation will beat with one pulse of joy and harmony. Throughout the enduring ages, we will worship and adore our generous God, the one who sacrificed everything so we could live.

Though the war is not yet over, it has already been won. God has won it by being himself, by being the kind of God who can be trusted. Even though he has already revealed this truth about the kind of person he is, he continues to wait.

He will wait until all his children have had the opportunity to make their choices. And every time one of us decides to trust him and come home, God wins the war all over again.

Let the good news about God be heard around the world: he is fully trustworthy. He is goodness and love personified. He treats all his creatures with graciousness and generosity. Now and for all eternity, we have *nothing to fear* from him who is love and life and freedom!

Appendix A

A picture of sin

We were created in God's image. That means we were designed to live as people who reflect his character. When sin entered our planet, we began living on the principles of selfishness, not love. What resulted is the world as we know it today.

Our little planet has become an example of what happens when people decide not to trust God and, instead, try to solve problems by "looking out for number one." For each of God's beautiful characteristics, there is an ugly alternative we find entrenched in our world.

Instead of God's oneness, we experience *alienation and estrangement*. This exists on a small scale (families) and a global scale (nations). This division leads to brokenness, as husbands and wives, families, groups, and nations turn on one another. Often, the unity we do see is contrived and short-lived.

Instead of God's life, we experience *death*. In a world of uncertainty, death is the only thing most people are certain of. Many of us also seek spiritual death. In small ways, we contribute every day to "little deaths" as we hurt others through our words, our actions, and our attitudes. We are selfish, not selfless.

Instead of God's honesty, we employ *dishonesty* when it's convenient. We lie to ourselves and each other. We don't see things as they really are, but as *we are*. This is why we are so eager to believe lies—especially the ones we tell ourselves.

Instead of God's power, we try to *grab power for ourselves*. We commonly abuse the power we acquire. "King of the hill" is not just a children's game. Individuals and nations struggle to acquire power, and then struggle to keep others from gaining or using power. Most people seek power as a substitute for character.

Instead of God's humility, we are plagued by *pride*. True humility is rare. We are obsessed with "my rights." Instead of the Father, Son, and Spirit, most people worship Me, Myself, and I.

Instead of God's holiness, most people seek after and celebrate what is *unholy*. Author Eugene Peterson put it best in his book *Run With the Horses*:

> People, aimless and bored, amuse themselves
> with trivia and trash. Neither the adventure of
> goodness nor the pursuit of righteousness gets
> headlines. . .

This condition has produced an odd phenomenon: individuals who live trivial lives and then engage in evil acts in order to establish significance for themselves. Assassins and hijackers attempt the gigantic leap from obscurity to fame by killing a prominent person or endangering the lives of an airplane full of passengers. Often they are successful.

The mass media report their words and display their actions. Writers vie with one another in analyzing their motives and providing psychological profiles on them. No other culture has been as eager to reward either nonsense or wickedness."*

Instead of God's orderliness, we mostly experience *chaos*. When individuals and groups act in self-interest, chaos and disorder is the result. Instead of caring about the needs of others, we will step on anyone we have to in order to get to "the top."

Instead of God's love, we hold up *lust* and call it "love." Acts of love designed by God have been reduced to self-seeking pleasure trips. True love is rare. In fact, we use the word "love" to describe everything except what it really is.

---

* Eugene H. Peterson, *Run With the Horses* (Downer's Grove: InterVarsity Press, 1983), 11.

Instead of God's friendship, we value *solitude*. Isolation is heralded as a way to avoid the pain of relationships. Today, the internet provides more "controlled" relationships—relating happens at one's whim with little face-to-face interaction.

Instead of God's giving, we *hoard* money and things. In the business world, this attitude is encouraged and even admired. The one who dies with the most toys wins.

Instead of God's truth-in-advertising, we *make unsubstantiated claims* about everything. From products to politics to our personal lives, we say what comes easily or what we want to believe instead of what is necessarily true. We base much of our lives on unsubstantiated claims—polls and statistics. As Mark Twain once said, "There are three kinds of lies: lies, damned lies, and statistics."

Instead of God's forgiveness, *revenge* is the near-universal human response to those who treat us poorly. Our "justice" is usually better defined as "getting even." This never satisfies us nor solves the problem.

Instead of God's initiation, we are usually on the *defensive*. Reaction is more common than action. This is how bad situations quickly escalate into tragedy. Instead of initiating good through action, we react without thinking.

Instead of God's patience, we treat others with *intolerance and impatience*. We have a hard time accepting the beliefs and opinions of others when they are different from ours. Especially in the age of high-speed technology, we can't be asked to wait for anything. Those who are slow to understand are ridiculed and treated as outcasts.

Instead of God's protectiveness, we value *self-preservation*. We believe that you have to "look out for number one." After all, if you don't look out for yourself, nobody else is going to, right? I *deserve* what's mine, and I have a right to get it!

Instead of God's self-assurance, *insecurity* plagues us. Those with fame and fortune have learned to mask it well, but our relationships with one another are infected with insecurity. Unsure of ourselves, we push others down and trample on them to secure our own position or make ourselves feel better.

Instead of God's wrath, we substitute *anger*. This anger is usually about self rather than others. When somebody hurts us, we feel angry. When somebody takes advantage of us, we want them to pay. Our anger is linked with our self-preservation. It almost never involves surrender of any kind on our part.

Instead of God's commitment to freedom, we value *subjection and conformity*. We say we value freedom, but we don't really respect those who make choices different from us. We want uniformity and control. We want others to submit to our authority, not exercise their freedom.

It's easy to see how character traits like these—multiplied on a global scale—can lead to a huge mess! There is a total breakdown of concern for our fellow human beings as we pursue what will exalt us or make us feel good. This is one of the reasons God allows the war to continue: to demonstrate what happens when people embrace selfishness instead of love.

The great news is that God is eager to restore his image in us. As we get to know him better, he removes our selfish tendencies and reignites our compassion and love for him, our fellow human beings, and ourselves.

Whenever and wherever that takes place in our world, we truly experience a little taste of heaven on Earth.

Notes

Chapter 1: The Universal War on Terror
1. See Rom. 6:23.
2. See Gen. 2:16-17.
3. See Gen. 3:10.

Chapter 2: Star Wars
1. Rev. 12:7 (New International Version, emphasis added).
2. Rev. 12:9, 12 (New Century Version).

Chapter 3: Battlefield Earth
1. Isa. 9:2 (NIV).
2. Isa. 9:2 (NIV).
3. John 1:5 (New Living Translation).
4. Luke 15:17 (NLT).

Chapter 4: If You've Seen One, You've Seen 'Em All
1. 1 Cor. 6:19 (NIV).
2. John 14:7, 9 (*Message*, emphasis added).
3. Deut. 6:4 (NIV).

4. Isa. 9:6 (NIV).
5. See John 16:26-27.

Chapter 5: Life Preserver

1. Rom. 6:23 (*Message*).

2. John 10:10 (NCV).
3. John 14:6 (NLT).
4. John 1:14 (NLT, emphasis added).
5. Ezek. 33:11 (NCV).
6. 1 Cor. 15:53 (NCV).
7. 1 Thess. 5:10 (*Message*).
8. See Rev. 2:11; 21:8.
9. Exod. 33:11 (NIV).
10. Exod. 34:29-30 (Today's New International Version, emphasis added).
11. Ezek. 18:31 (*Message*).

Chapter 6: Reality Show

1. See Gen. 2:17.
2. See Rev. 12:9.
3. Gen. 3:4-5 (TNIV).
4. Rom. 3:25-26, paraphrased.
5. See Mark 15:34.
6. See Luke 22:44; Mark 14:33-34.
7. Gen. 2:17 (NCV).
8. Max Lucado, *In the Eye of the Storm* (Dallas: Word Publishing, 1991), 35-37.
9. Matt. 27:46 (*Message*).
10. See 2 Cor. 5:21.
11. John 14:6 (NIV).

Chapter 7: Higher Power
1. See Ps. 33:6.
2. See Job 38:8-11.
3. See Josh. 10:13.
4. See John 2:1-10.
5. Ps. 33:6,9 (NIV).
6. See 2 Cor. 12:9.
7. Phil. 4:13 (NCV).

Chapter 8: Heads or Tails
1. Isa. 53:3-4, 7-8 (NCV).
2. See Matt. 8:26-27.
3. See John 11:43-44.
4. See John 18:4-6.
5. See Luke 22:50-51.
6. See John 15:15.
7. See Mark 9:33-35.
8. *Schindler's List*, VHS, directed by Stephen Spielberg (Hollywood, CA: Universal Studios: 1993).
9. Matt. 23:11-12 (NCV).
10. Phil. 2:5-11 (NCV).

Chapter 9: O Holy Knight
1. See 1 Tim. 6:16.
2. See John 1:4.
3. See John 1:3.
4. See 2 Cor. 6:14-15.
5. Isa 6:1-7 (NLT).
6. See Gen. 1:26.
7. See Isa. 1:18.
8. Isa. 6:9 (NCV).

Chapter 10: The Deity is in the Details
1. See Ps. 139:14.
2. 1 Cor. 12:14-20 (NLT).
3. See Rom. 1:20.

Chapter 11: What's Love Got to Do With It?
1. Michael W. Smith and Wayne Kirkpatrick, "The Other Side of Me," © 1995 O'Ryan Music Inc.
2. 1 John 4:7-8 (NCV).
3. 1 Cor. 13:1-7 (NCV).
4. See Luke 15:21-22.
5. John 3:16 (NIV).
6. See 1 Cor. 13:8.

Chapter 12: Man's Best Friend
1. John 15:15 (NLT).
2. Gen. 18:20-25 (NCV).
3. Num. 14:13, 15-16 (NIV).
4. Jon. 4:1-2 (*Message*).
5. A. Graham Maxwell, *Servants or Friends?* (Redlands: Pine Knoll Publications, 2002), 43.

Chapter 13: Giving it All He's Got
1. James 1:17 (*Message*).
2. See Exod. 17:6.
3. See Exod. 16:13-15.
4. See Exod. 13:21-22.
5. 1 Kings 17:6 (NIV).
6. See Matt. 10:29.
7. See Gen. 3:7.
8. See Gen. 3:21.

9. 1 John 3:20 (NIV).

10. 1 John 3:19 (NIV).

11. Deut. 6:10-12 (NCV, emphasis added).

12. Matt. 5:43-48 (*Message*, emphasis added).

13. Ron Harris and Claire Cloninger, "The Gift Goes On," © 1983 Ron Harris Music.

Chapter 14: Show Business

1. See Gen. 3:4.

2. See Matt. 27:40.

3. See Luke 23:34.

4. See John 19:25-27.

5. See Luke 23:43.

6. See Gen. 3:5.

7. See Gen. 3:4.

8. See Rom. 3:25-26.

9. 2 Cor. 5:21 (NCV).

10. Matt. 27:46 (NLT).

11. See Rom. 6:23.

Chapter 15: God Must Be Odd, 'Cuz He Never Gets Even

1. See Luke 15:11-32.

2. Luke 15:20 (NIV).

3. See Matt. 26:69-75.

4. See Mark 16:7.

5. See John 8:4-5.

6. See John 8:11.

7. See Rev. 3:8; 4:1.

8. See Rev. 20:10; Matt. 25:41.

9. Rom. 12:18-21 (*Message*).

Chapter 16: Look Who's Stalking
1. Gen 3:9 (NIV).
2. Hosea 3:1 (*Message*).
3. John 1:14 (NIV, emphasis added).
4. Ps. 139:7-10 (NCV).

Chapter 17: Heaven Can Wait
1. See Matt. 7:1.
2. Phil. 1:6 (NCV).
3. Heb. 12:2 (NLT).
4. John 16:12 (NCV).

Chapter 18: On Guard
1. See Deut. 5:17.
2. See Deut. 21:1-9.
3. See Deut. 15:1.
4. See Num. 11:4-6.
5. Matt. 5:17 (NLT).
6. See Matt. 22:38-39.
7. Gal. 3:23 (TNIV).
8. See 1 Pet. 5:8.
9. See Gen. 2:2-3.
10. See Exod. 20:8-11.
11. See Deut. 5:15.
12. See Mark 2:27.
13. Elisabeth Elliot, *Passion and Purity* (Ada: Revell, 2002), 85.
14. Isa. 43:2 (NLV).
15. 1 Thess. 5:18 (NIV).

Chapter 19: Frequently Asked Questions
1. See John 15:15.
2. Job 13:22 (NLV).
3. Dan. 9:22-23 (NLT).
4. See Isa. 1:18.
5. See Rom. 9:30.
6. Mark 12:14-17 (NCV).

Chapter 20: Unconditional Surrender
1. C.S. Lewis, *The Great Divorce* (New York: HarperOne, 2001), 75.
2. See Rom. 1:18-32.
3. See Rom 4:25.
4. See Isa. 28:21.
5. Hos. 11:8, paraphrased.
6. See Rom. 1:24, 26, 28.
7. See Rev. 22:11.

Chapter 21: Keeping Our Options Open
1. See Ezek. 33:11.
2. See Josh. 24:15.